A-Z FOLKESTO... DEAL &

CW00501015

CONTENT...

REFERENCE

Motorway	M20	**Local Authority Boundary**	
A Road	A20	**Posttown Boundary**	
Under Construction		**Postcode Boundary** Within Posttown	
Proposed		**Map Continuation**	8
B Road	B2011	**Car Park** selected	P
Dual Carriageway		**Cycle Route**	
Tunnel	A20	**Church or Chapel**	†
One Way Street Traffic flow on A Roads is indicated by a heavy line on the drivers' left.	→	**Fire Station**	■
		Hospital	H
Pedestrianized Road		**House Numbers** A & B Roads only	79 24
Restricted Access			
Track		**Information Centre**	🛈
Footpath		**National Grid Reference**	630
Residential Walkway		**Police Station**	▲
Railway	Tunnel / Station / Level Crossing	**Post Office**	★
		Toilet	▽
Built Up Area	HIGH STREET	**with facilities for the Disabled**	♿

SCALE   1:15,840   4 Inches to 1 Mile or 6.31 cm to 1 Km

0	¼	½	¾	1 Mile

0	250	500	750 Metres	1 Kilometre

Copyright of Geographers' A-Z Map Company Ltd.

Head Office:
Fairfield Road, Borough Green, Sevenoaks, Kent TN15 8PP
Telephone 01732 781000 (General Enquiries & Trade Sales)
Showrooms:
44 Gray's Inn Road, London WC1X 8HX
Telephone 020 7440 9500 (Retail Sales)
www.a-zmaps.co.uk

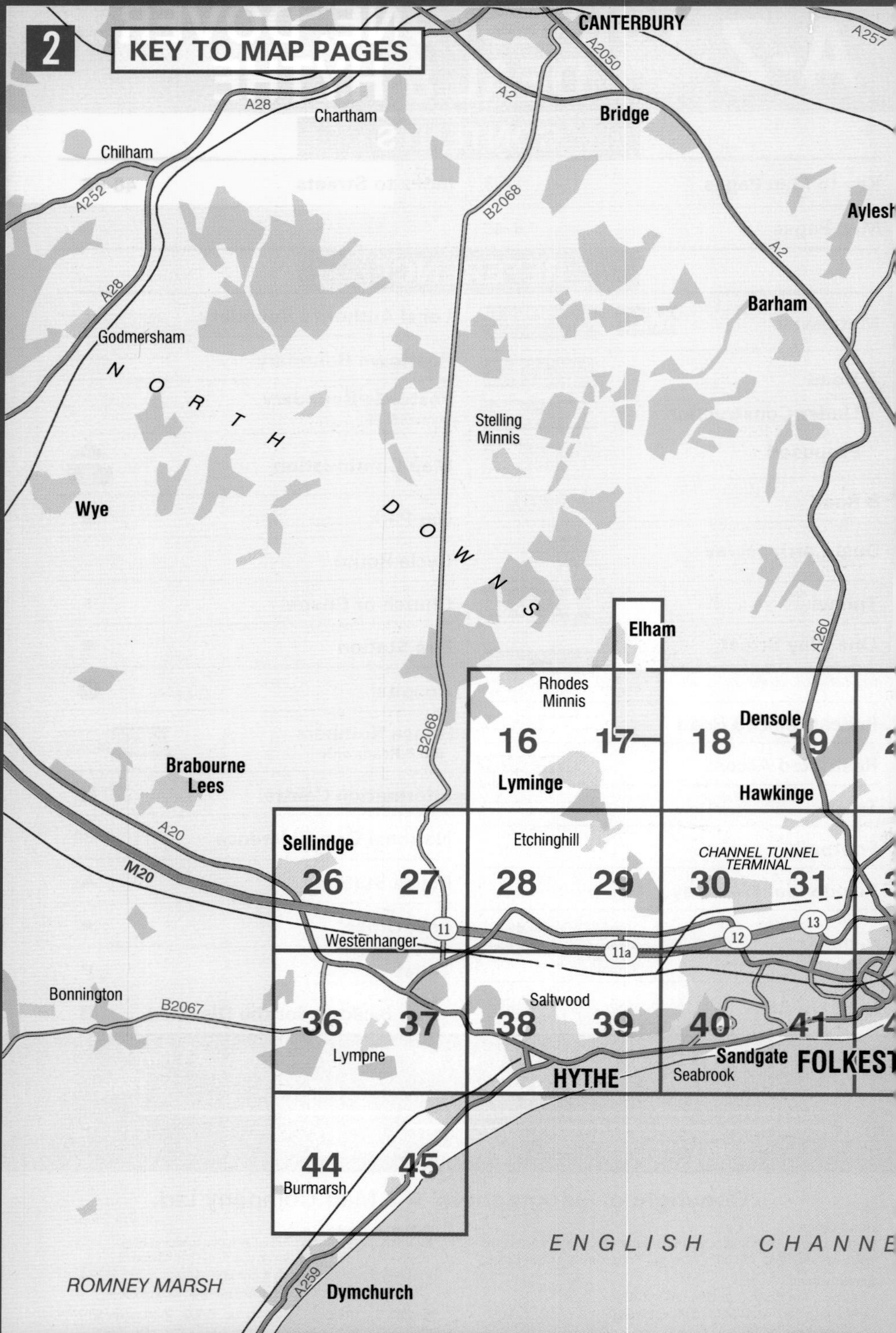

2 KEY TO MAP PAGES

CANTERBURY

A257

A2050

A28

Chartham

Bridge

Chilham

A252

B2068

A2

Aylesh

Godmersham

Barham

N O R T H

Stelling
Minnis

Wye

D O W N S

A260

Elham

Rhodes
Minnis

Densole

B2068

16   17   18   19   2

Brabourne
Lees

Lyminge

Hawkinge

Sellindge

Etchinghill

A20

CHANNEL TUNNEL
TERMINAL

M20

26   27   28   29   30   31   3

Westenhanger   11   11a   12   13

Bonnington   B2067

Saltwood

36   37   38   39   40   41   4

Lympne

Sandgate   FOLKEST

HYTHE   Seabrook

44   45

Burmarsh

E N G L I S H   C H A N N E

ROMNEY MARSH   A259   Dymchurch

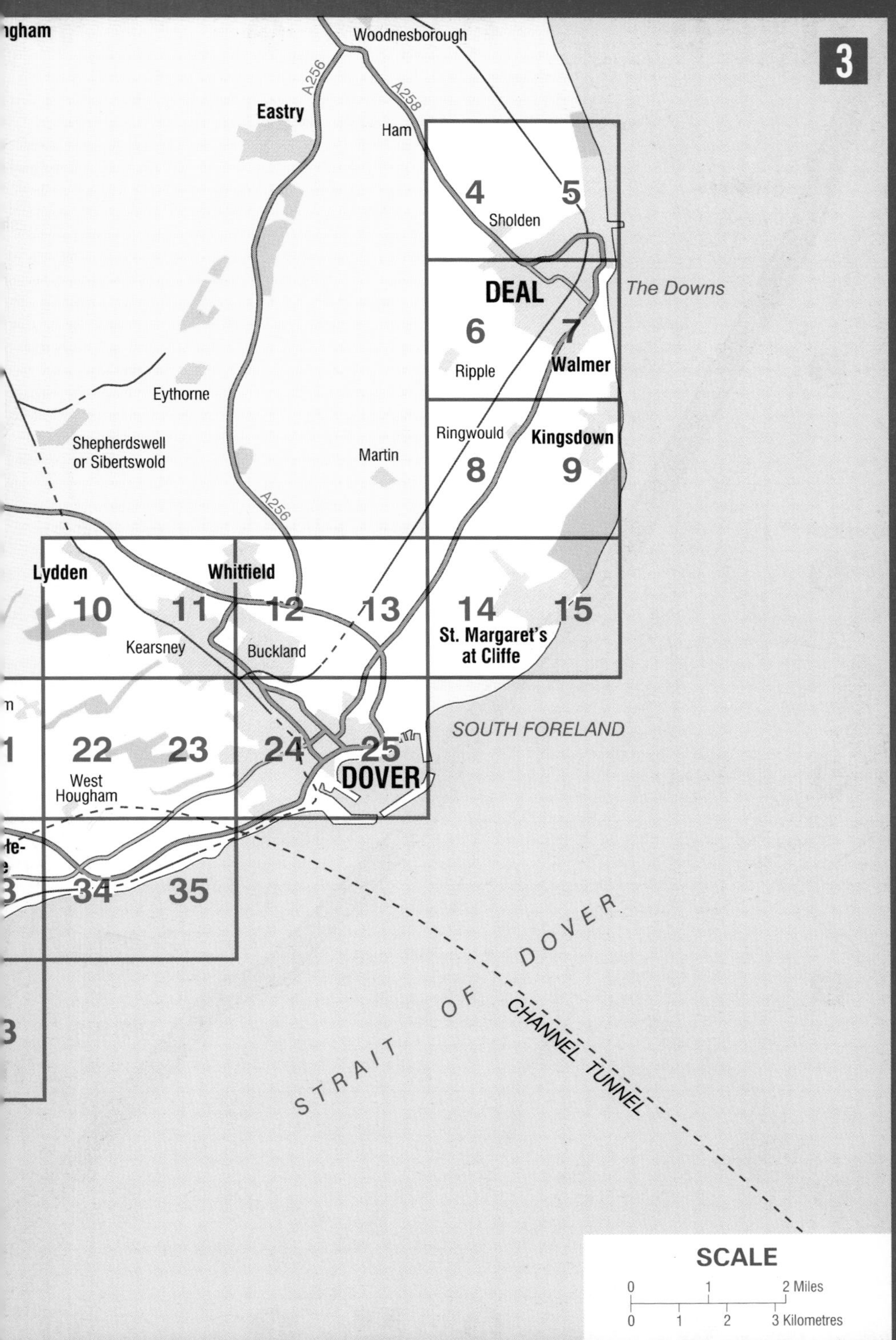

ngham

Woodnesborough

Eastry

A256

A258

Ham

4 **5**

Sholden

DEAL The Downs

6 **7**

Ripple **Walmer**

Ringwould **Kingsdown**

Martin **8** **9**

Eythorne

Shepherdswell
or Sibertswold

A256

Lydden **Whitfield**

10 **11** **12** **13** **14** **15**

Kearsney Buckland St. Margaret's
at Cliffe

n SOUTH FORELAND

22 **23** **24** **25**
West **DOVER**
Hougham

te- **34** **35**
e
3

STRAIT OF DOVER

OF CHANNEL TUNNEL

3

SCALE

0   1   2 Miles

0   1   2   3 Kilometres

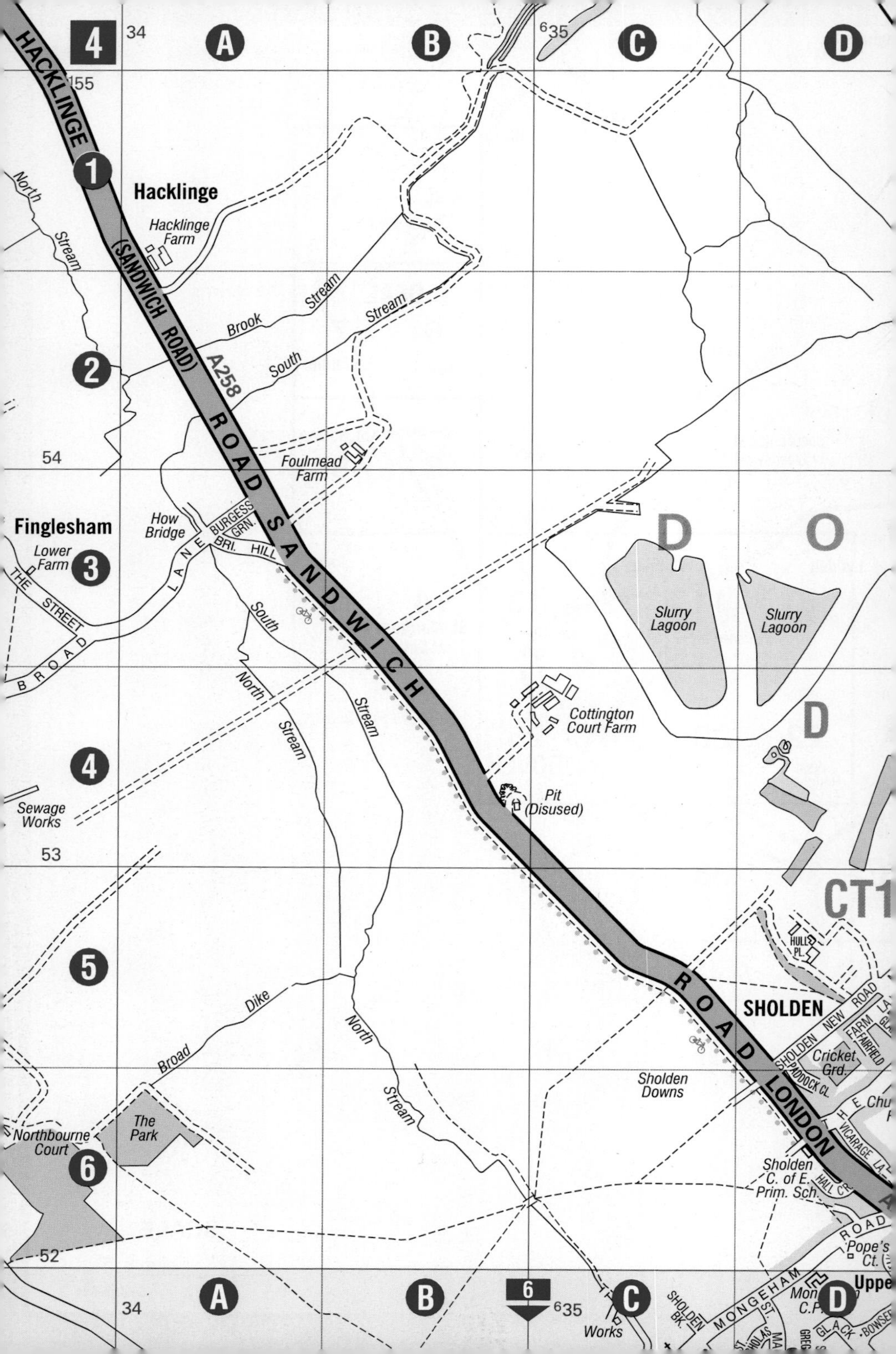
A
B
C
D
34
635
155
HACKLINGE
(SANDWICH ROAD)
A258
Hacklinge
Hacklinge Farm
North Stream
Brook Stream
South Stream
ROAD
SANDWICH
Foulmead Farm
54
Finglesham
How Bridge
BURGESS GRN.
BRI. HILL
LANE
Lower Farm
THE STREET
BROAD
South
North Stream
Stream
Cottington Court Farm
Pit (Disused)
D
O
D
Slurry Lagoon
Slurry Lagoon
Sewage Works
53
CT1
HULLS PL.
SHOLDEN
SHOLDEN NEW ROAD
FARM
FAIRFIELD
Cricket Grd.
PADDOCK CL.
Broad Dike
North Stream
ROAD
LONDON
Sholden Downs
The Park
Northbourne Court
Sholden C. of E. Prim. Sch.
VICARAGE LA.
HALL
ROAD
Pope's Ct.
MONGEHAM
SHOLDEN BK.
52
Works
1
2
3
4
5
6

6

5
E
F
G
H
37
38
55
54
53
52
1
2
3
4
5
6
Tennants Hills
ROYAL CINQUE PORTS GOLF COURSE
Walnut Tree Farm
Golf House
Club Ho.
South London Family Camp
REDHOUSE
REDHOUSE LA.
REDHOUSE BUNGALOWS
WALL
Barns Close
Redhouse Barn
Sandown Castle (Rems. of)
Sewer
NORTHWALL
ROAD
SOUTH
LANE
Kennels Farm
Sandfield Farm
Groynes
ETHELBERT RD.
GODWYN RD.
HAROLD ROAD
GOLF CT.
VLISSINGEN DR.
BECKET
COURTENAY RD.
MILLER CL.
LINKS
THE FAIRWAY
WEST
CANNON STREET
NORTHWALL
Sch.
ARK LA.
ROAD
PETER ST.
WATER ST.
GERALD PALMBY CT.
Play. Fld.
Pav.
Works
DEAL
MINTRES IND. EST.
SOUTHWALL
ROAD
Play. Fld.
Brambles Nursery Sch.
CHURCH PATH
Deal
QUEEN ST.
ROAD
A258
Prim. Sch.
Middle Deal
Bowl. Grn.
Youth Cen.
Victoria Pk.
Health Cen.
VICTORIA HOSP.
PARK
AVENUE
GILFORD
Leisure Pool
RAVENSCOURT
Recreation
Playing Field
LONDON
Warden Ho. C.P.Sch.
Drill Hall
DOLA AVENUE
CHURCH
ORCHARD AV.
MIDDLE DEAL
VICTORIA ROAD
THE STRAND
MARINE RD.
Deal Castle
VICTORIA PARADE
PRINCE OF WALES TERRACE
BEECHWOOD AV.
Mus.
Leis. Cen.
Royal Hotel
Promenade Pier
PROMENADE
NORTH
BEACH
SOUTH
MARINA
7
37
38

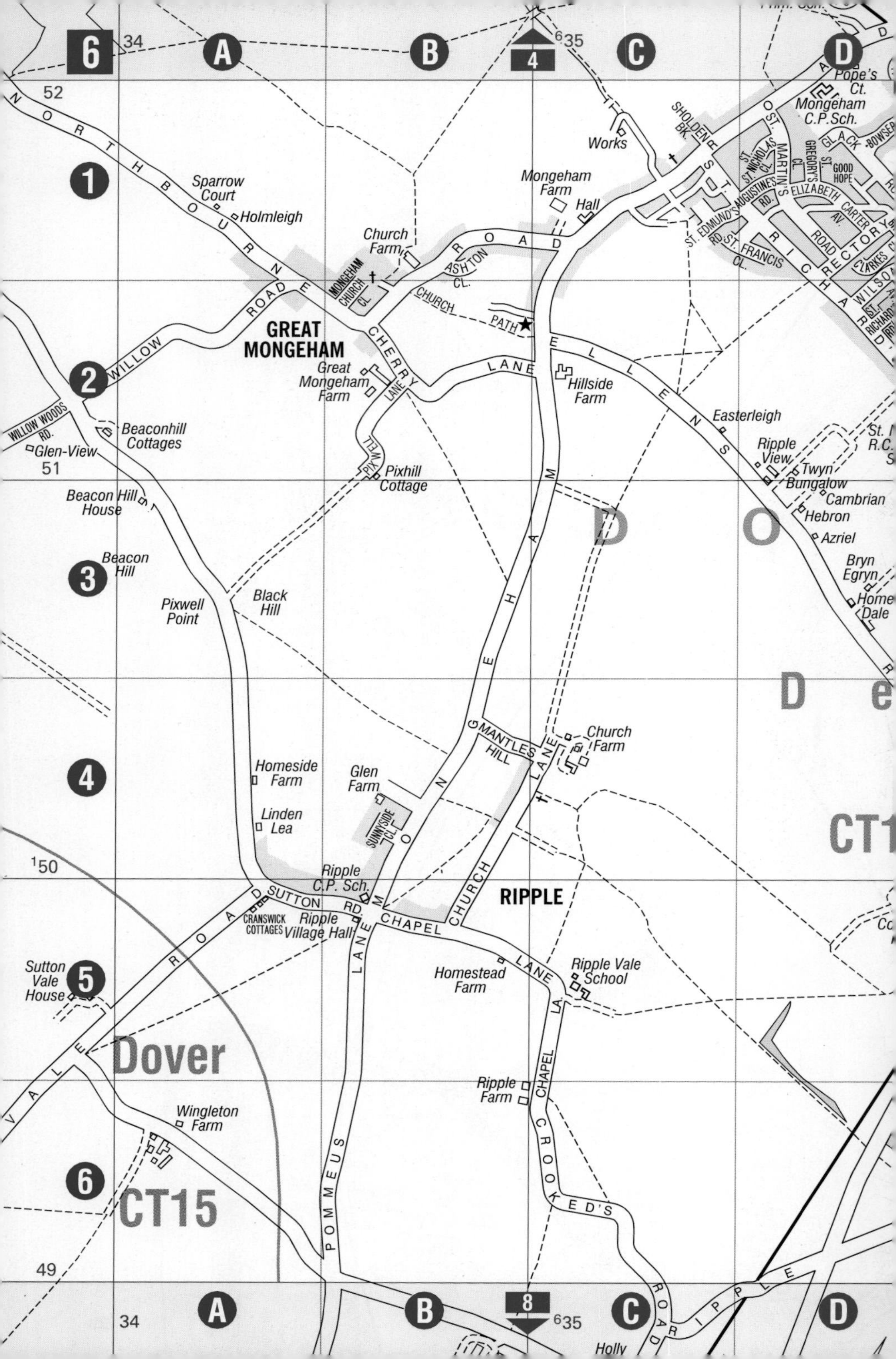
6
GREAT MONGEHAM
RIPPLE
Dover
CT15
NORTHBOURNE ROAD
WILLOW ROAD
CHERRY LANE
MONGEHAM ROAD
ELLENS ROAD
SUTTON ROAD
CHAPEL LANE
CHURCH LANE
POMMEUS LANE
CROOKED'S ROAD
RIPPLE ROAD
MANTLES HILL
CHURCH PATH
ASHTON CL.
MONGEHAM CHURCH CL.
SUNNYSIDE CL.
PIXWELL LANE
WILLOW WOODS RD.
VALE
CRANSWICK COTTAGES
Sparrow Court
Holmleigh
Church Farm
Mongeham Farm
Hall
Works
Great Mongeham Farm
Hillside Farm
Beaconhill Cottages
Glen-View
Beacon Hill House
Beacon Hill
Pixhill Cottage
Pixwell Point
Black Hill
Easterleigh
Ripple View
Twyn Bungalow
Cambrian
Hebron
Azriel
Bryn Egryn
Home Dale
Homeside Farm
Linden Lea
Glen Farm
Ripple C.P. Sch.
Ripple Village Hall
Homestead Farm
Ripple Vale School
Ripple Farm
Sutton Vale House
Wingleton Farm
Holly
Pope's Ct.
Mongeham C.P.Sch.
SHOLDEN BK.
ST. NICHOLAS CL.
ST. MARTIN'S CL.
GREGORY'S CL.
ST. AUGUSTINE'S RD.
ST. EDMUND'S RD.
ST. FRANCIS CL.
ELIZABETH CARTER AV.
GOOD HOPE
RECTORY
RICHARD RD.
WILSON
ST. RICHARDS
CLARKES CL.
GLACK
BOWSER
St. M R.C. S
D O
D e
CT1
4
8
34
635
52
51
150
49

DEAL
WALMER
Upper Walmer
Lower Walmer
MILL HILL
Hawksdown
Recreation Ground
Playing Field
Deal Town F.C.
Castle Community Sch.
South Deal Co. Prim. Sch.
Cemetery
Miniature Golf Course
Marke Wood Rec. Grd.
The Downs C. of E. Prim. School
Walmer School
Walmer Riding Centre
Clifford Park Caravan Site
Meadowside Training Cen.
Liverpool House
Walmer Castle
Hawks Hill House
Hawkshill Down
Hawkshill Farm
Hawkshill Camp
The Firs
Rays Bottom
King's Farm
Claytons Hill
Deal Castle
Water Wks.
VICTORIA HOSP.
THE STRAND
DOVER ROAD
HAMILTON RD.
CORNWALL RD.
MANOR ROAD
MILL RD.
LIVERPOOL ROAD
WELLINGTON PARADE
GRANVILLE ROAD
SALISBURY ROAD
CANADA ROAD
HAWKSDOWN
A258
B2056
PROMENADE
E
F
G
H
1
2
3
4
5
6
5
9
37
38
49
50
51
52

8
34
A
B
6
635
C
D
49
48
147
46
1
2
3
4
5
6
POMMEUS LA.
CROOKED'S RD.
RIPPLE
Holly Lodge
Tennis Ct.
Ripple Court
Brathay
Wind Pump
Ripple Cross
SUTTON
Manor Fm.
LA.
The Forest
HANGMAN'S LA.
BACK
QUEEN'S RISE
Westfields
Winklandoaks Farm
Winklandoaks Cottages
HANGMAN'S
Subway
LANE
D O
DOVER
ROAD
RINGWOULD
Appleton Manor
Dover
Longclose Wood
Follyclose Wood
WATERWORKS LA.
Martin Farm
THE STREET
Martin Lodge
MARTIN
LUCERNE
Oxneybottom Wood
Old Wood
CT15
Hollands Hill
Martin Mill
MARTIN DALE CR.
LANE
STA. APP.
BARLEY C.
Oxney Court
Play Fld.
OLD ROMAN RD.
STATION
MARTIN MILL
A258
Martin Vale
GURLING
BERESFORD
GREEN
VICTORY
NELSON
ROAD
14

9
7
37
38
15
E
F
G
H
1
2
3
4
5
6
49
48
47
46
Hawkshill Camp
Claytons Hill
Knights Bottom
Knights Hill
St. Nicholas & St. John's C. of E. Prim. Sch.
The Butts
Hall
RINGWOULD ROAD
NGWOULD
A258
DEAL ROAD
GLEN ROAD
CLAREMONT C.
CLAREMONT RD.
OSBOURNE RD.
BALMORAL ROAD
EDWARD RD.
CARLTON RD.
SEA ROAD
KING'S CLOSE
CLIM DOWN
ST. MONICA'S RD.
CHURCH CLIFF
CLIFFE ROAD
KINGSDOWN RD.
COURTLANDS
BOUNDARY RD.
JARVIST PL.
NORTH RD.
SOUTH RD.
WELLINGTON PARADE
Mean High Water
Mean Low Water
THE RISE
UPPER STREET
ST. JAMES RD.
ALEXANDRA RD.
CHALK HILL RD.
THE ROAD
Chalk Hill Farm
KINGSDOWN
Kingsdown Holiday Camp
Scout Camp
THE AVENUE
UNDERCLIFFE ROAD
Woodhill Farm
Great Coombe
Wood Hill
Kingsdown Wood (N.T.)
KINGSDOWN ROAD
HILLCREST ROAD
QUEENSDOWN
BAYVIEW ROAD
VICTORIA ROAD
NORTHCOTE RD.
HILL ROAD
COASTGUARD COTTS.
Rifle Range
Oldstairs Bay
Club House
THE LEAS ROAD
The Swamp
Old Parker's Cap
E R
Deal
Lynch
Hill Farm
Barrows Hill
East Bottom Farm
East Bottom Road
GRANVILLE ROAD
WALMER AND KINGSDOWN GOLF COURSE
The Leas (N.T.)
CT14
OLDSTAIRS
Otty Bottom
Otty Bottom Cottage
Kent Bridge House
South Foreland House
Hope Point House
Hope Bay Studios
THE LEAS
Free Down
East Hill
COLLINGWOOD ROAD EAST
Old Bottom Free Down
Barrow Mount
THE LEAS NATIONAL TRUST AREA
NORWAY DROVE

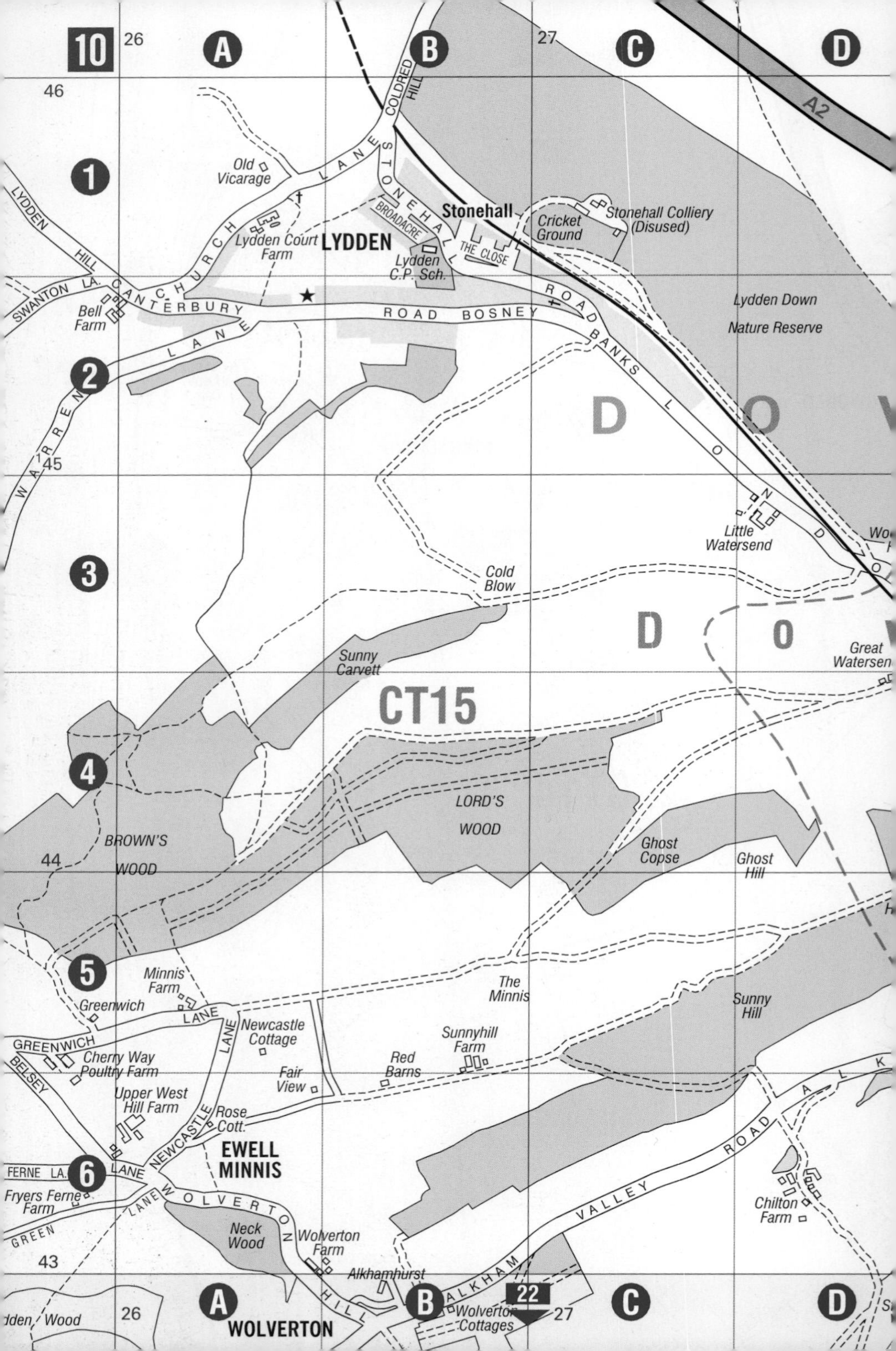

A
B
C
D
26
27
46
45
44
43
1
2
3
4
5
6
A2
COLDRED HILL
CHURCH LANE
STONEHALL
BROADACRE
THE CLOSE
Stonehall
Old Vicarage
Stonehall Colliery (Disused)
Cricket Ground
Lydden Court Farm
LYDDEN
Lydden C.P. Sch.
LYDDEN HILL
SWANTON LA.
Bell Farm
CANTERBURY ROAD
ROAD BOSNEY
Lydden Down
Nature Reserve
LANE
WARREN LANE
BANKS LONDON ROAD
D O
Little Watersend
Cold Blow
Sunny Carvett
CT15
Great Watersen
LORD'S WOOD
BROWN'S WOOD
Ghost Copse
Ghost Hill
Minnis Farm
Greenwich
The Minnis
Sunny Hill
GREENWICH LANE
Newcastle Cottage
Cherry Way Poultry Farm
Sunnyhill Farm
Red Barns
Fair View
BELSEY
Upper West Hill Farm
Rose Cott.
NEWCASTLE LANE
EWELL MINNIS
FERNE LA.
Fryers Ferne Farm
GREEN LANE
WOLVERTON HILL
Neck Wood
Wolverton Farm
ALKHAM VALLEY ROAD
Chilton Farm
Alkhamhurst
22
Wolverton Cottages
dden Wood
WOLVERTON

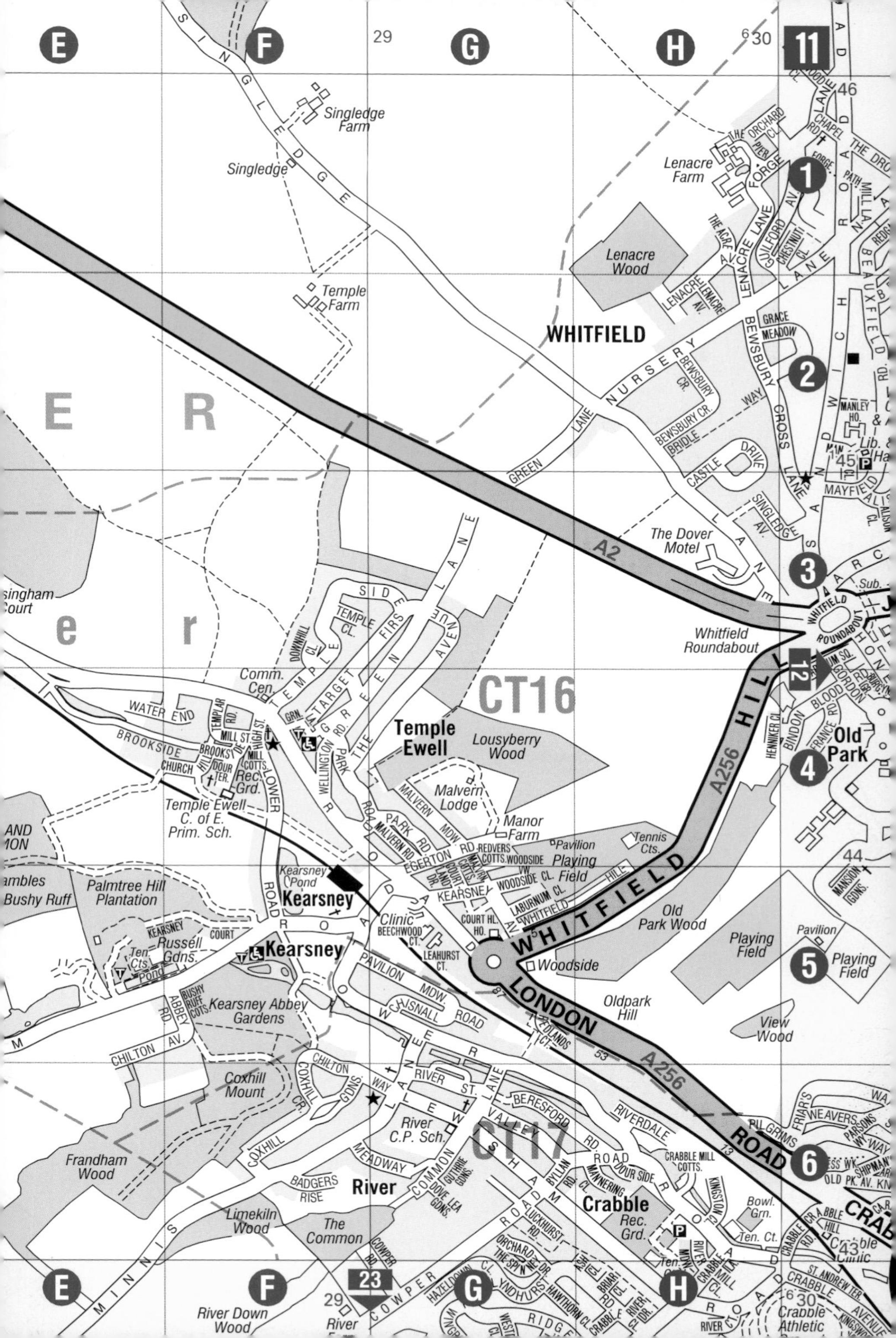
E
F
G
H
29
630
Singledge Farm
Singledge
SINGLEDGE
Temple Farm
WHITFIELD
Lenacre Farm
Lenacre Wood
NURSERY
BEWSBURY CROSS LANE
GREEN LANE
A2
The Dover Motel
Whitfield Roundabout
CT16
Temple Ewell
Lousyberry Wood
Malvern Lodge
Manor Farm
Pavilion
Playing Field
Tennis Cts.
WHITFIELD HILL
A256
Old Park
Old Park Wood
Playing Field
Pavilion
Playing Field
View Wood
Oldpark Hill
LONDON ROAD
A256
Kearsney
Kearsney Pond
Clinic
Woodside
Palmtree Hill Plantation
Russell Gdns.
Kearsney Abbey Gardens
Coxhill Mount
Frandham Wood
Limekiln Wood
The Common
River
River C.P. Sch.
CT17
Crabble
Crabble Rec. Grd.
Crabble Athletic
River Down Wood
Temple Ewell C. of E. Prim. Sch.
Comm. Cen.
PILGRIMS
ROAD
23
12
43
44
45
46
53
73
MINNIS
COWPER
RIDGE
WATER END
BROOKSIDE
CHURCH
LOWER ROAD
KEARSNEY COURT
CHILTON AV.
COXHILL CR.
MEADWAY
BADGERS RISE
RIVER ST.
VALLEY RD.
BERESFORD RD.
RIVERDALE
SHAM ROAD
EGERTON RD.
PARK RD.
MALVERN MDW.
WELLINGTON RD.
TEMPLE SIDE
TEMPLE CL.
FIRS
THE GREEN
TARGET
CASTLE DRIVE
BRIDLE WAY
BEWSBURY CR.
SINGLEDGE AV.
SINGLEDGE LANE
LENACRE LANE
LENACRE AV.
GRACE MEADOW
CHESTNUT CL.
GUILFORD AV.
FORGE
BLOOD
GORDON RD.
FRANCE RD.
BINDON
HENNIKER CL.
MANSION GDNS.
FRIAR'S
WEAVERS
PARSONS WY.
OLD PK AV.
CRABBLE AVENUE
CRABBLE MILL COTTS.
KINGSTON CL.
LUCKHURST RD.
HAZELDOWN CL.
LYNDHURST
WHITFIELD ROUNDABOUT
MAYFIELD
SANDWICH ROAD
BEAUXFIELD
MANLEY HO.
REDLANDS CT.
PAVILION MDW.
LEAHURST CT.
BEECHWOOD CT.
WOODSIDE CL.
LABURNUM CL.
KEARSNEY AV.
COURT HL. HO.

12
A
B
C
D
1
2
3
4
5
6
630
31
46
45
44
43
Church Whitfield
WHITFIELD
Little Pineham Farm
Pineham
Parsonage Farm
Lenacre Farm
Rec. Grd.
Old People's Home
Whitfield C.P. Sch. & Aspen Unit
Lib. & Hall
Dover Motel
CT16
A2
JUBILEE
A256
Whitfield Roundabout
WHITFIELD ROUNDABOUT
11
HILL
Training Cen.
Council Offs.
DOVER BUSINESS PARK
Superstores
PARKWAY
White Cliffs Bus. Pk.
Refuse Transfer Sta.
(Proposed)
Old Pk. Wood
Old Park
Dover Transport Museum
Running Track
Playing Field
Archers Court School
Old Park Barracks
MELBOURNE AVENUE
WHITFIELD
Wood
Playing Field
Pavilion
Playing Field
View Wood
The Powell Co. Prim. School
Melbourne C.P. Sch.
Green La. Hill
Sports Ground
Buckland Valley
Buckland
Whiting Poultry Farm
Playing Field
ROMAN ROAD
BARNTYE
LONDON RD.
CRABBLE HL.
Crabble Clinic
Crabble Athletic
Bowl. Grn.
Ten. Ct.
24
The Da Rec.
Charlton Cemetery
D
O
D
O
NURSERY
LENACRE LANE
FORGE LANE
THE DROVE
NAPCHESTER
SANDWICH
BEAUXFIELD
ALISON CRESCENT
ARCHERS COURT
NEWLANDS
HONEYWOOD
CRANLEIGH
FARNCOMBE WAY
JOYES RD.
MAYFIELD
SINGLEDGE AV.
BEWSBURY CROSS LA.
GRACE MEADOW
OLD PARK HILL
CHURCH WHITFIELD ROAD
PINEHAM
PILGRIMS WAY
CHAUCER CRESCENT
WINANT WAY
GREEN LANE
LINCES
DURBAN CRESCENT
KIMBERLEY CL.
DR. AUCKLAND
DUNEDIN
HOBART CRES.
FULBERT RD.
ROKESLEY RD.
HIRST CL.
COLTON CRES.
ROOSEVELT
KNIGHTS

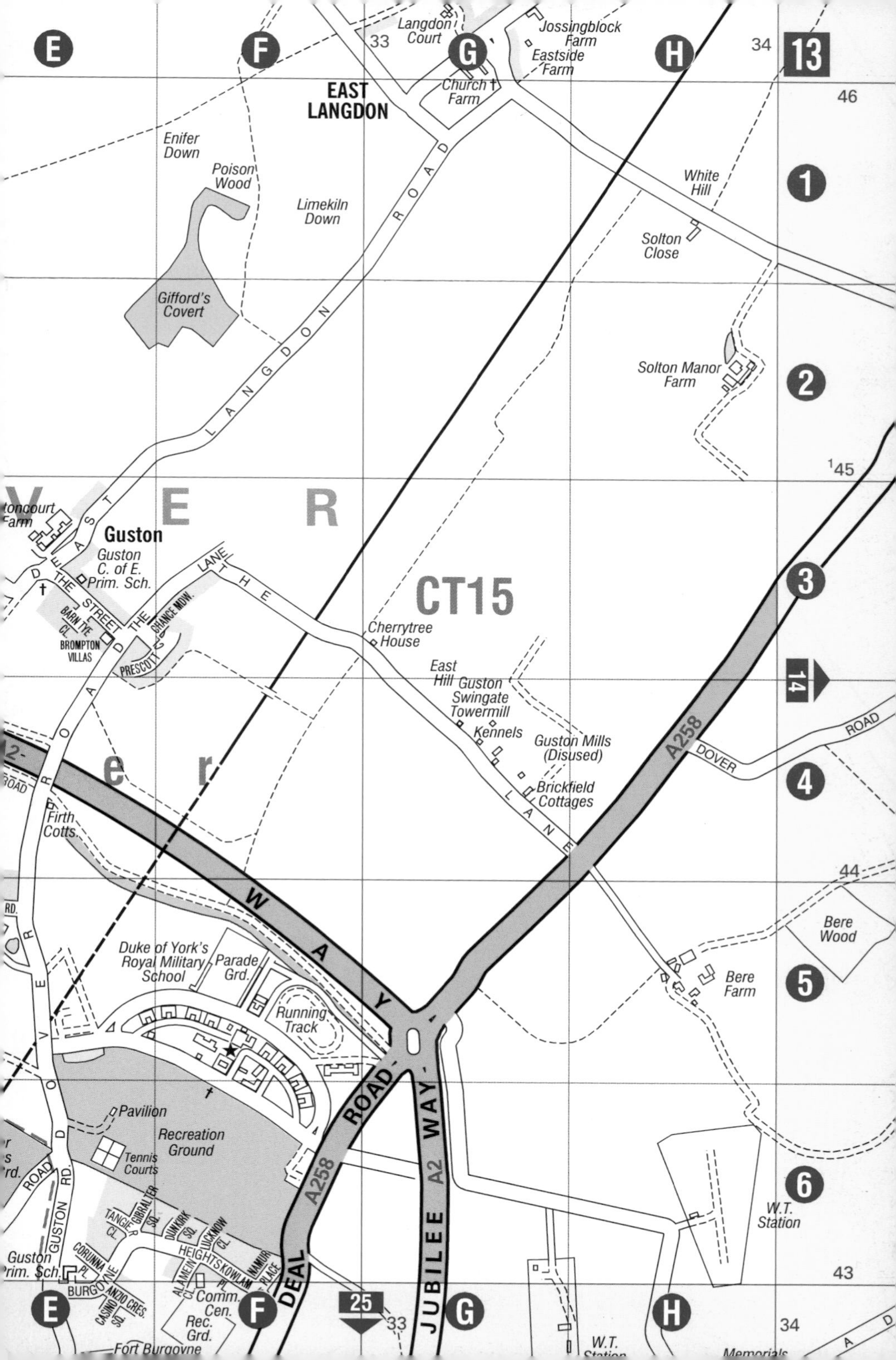

E   **F**   **G**   **H**   34   **13**

46

Langdon
Court

Jossingblock
Farm
Eastside
Farm

33

EAST
LANGDON

Church
Farm

Enifer
Down

White
Hill

1

Poison
Wood

Limekiln
Down

Solton
Close

L
A
N
G
D
O
N

R
O
A
D

Gifford's
Covert

Solton Manor
Farm

2

¹45

V   E   R

oncourt
Farm

Guston

3

Guston
C. of E.
Prim. Sch.

LANE

THE

CT15

Cherrytree
House

GRANGE MDW.

PRESCOTT

THE STREET

BARN TYE
CL.

BROMPTON
VILLAS

East
Hill

Guston
Swingate
Towermill

14

Kennels

Guston Mills
(Disused)

DOVER

A258

ROAD

4

Brickfield
Cottages

Firth
Cotts.

LANE

44

Bere
Wood

RD.

Duke of York's
Royal Military
School

Parade
Grd.

Bere
Farm

5

Running
Track

W
A
Y

ROAD

2-

Pavilion

Recreation
Ground

Tennis
Courts

A258

ROAD

A2 WAY

6

W.T.
Station

Guston
Prim. Sch.

GUSTON RD.

TANGIER SQ.
CORUNNA

GIBRALTAR SQ.
SUDK
BURGOYNE

CASSINO SQ.
ANZIO CRES.

HEIGHTS
ALAMEIN

VIMY SQ.
INKERMAN
SOMME

KOWLMN CL.

E   **F**   **25**   33   **G**   **H**   34

43

Comm.
Cen.
Rec.
Grd.

Fort Burgoyne

DEAL   ROAD

JUBILEE

W.T.
Station

Memorials

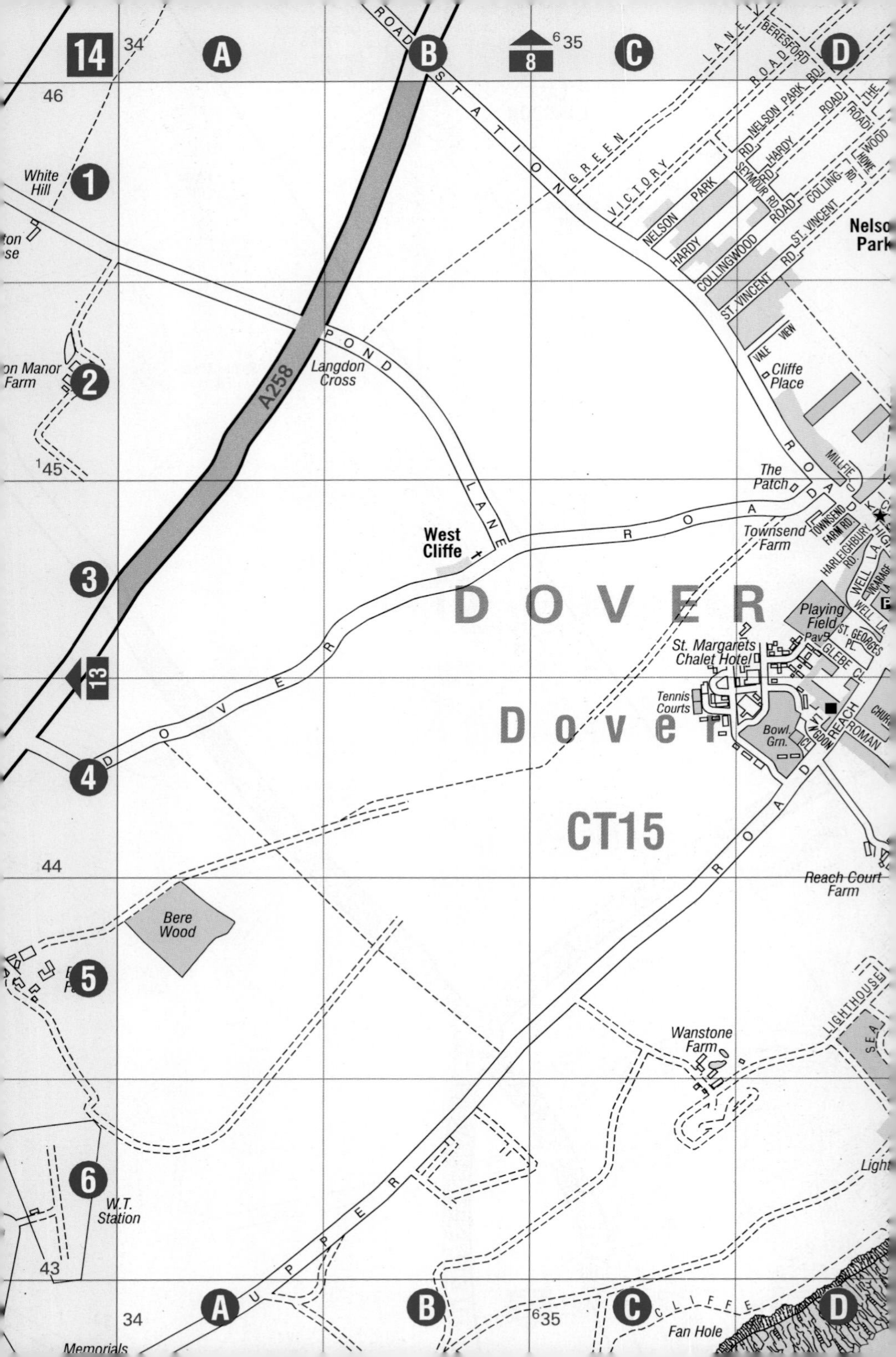
A
B
C
D
1
2
3
4
5
6
34
6 35
46
145
44
43
8
13
White Hill
Langdon Cross
West Cliffe
DOVER
Dover
CT15
A258
STATION ROAD
POND LANE
DOVER ROAD
UPPER ROAD
GREEN LANE
VICTORY ROAD
BERESFORD
NELSON PARK RD.
NELSON PARK
HARDY
COLLINGWOOD
ST. VINCENT
ST. VINCENT RD.
SEYMOUR RD.
HARDY ROAD
COLLING-WOOD RD.
THE ROAD
HOWE
VALE VIEW
Cliffe Place
MILLFIELD
The Patch
Townsend Farm
TOWNSEND FARM RD.
HARLEIGHBURY RD.
HIGH
WELL LA.
VICARAGE LA.
WELL LA.
Playing Field
Pav.
ST. GEORGES PL.
GLEBE CL.
St. Margarets Chalet Hotel
Tennis Courts
Bowl. Grn.
REACH
ROMAN
CHURCH
Reach Court Farm
Bere Wood
Wanstone Farm
LIGHTHOUSE
SEA
W.T. Station
CLIFFE
Fan Hole
Memorials
Nelson Park
Manor Farm

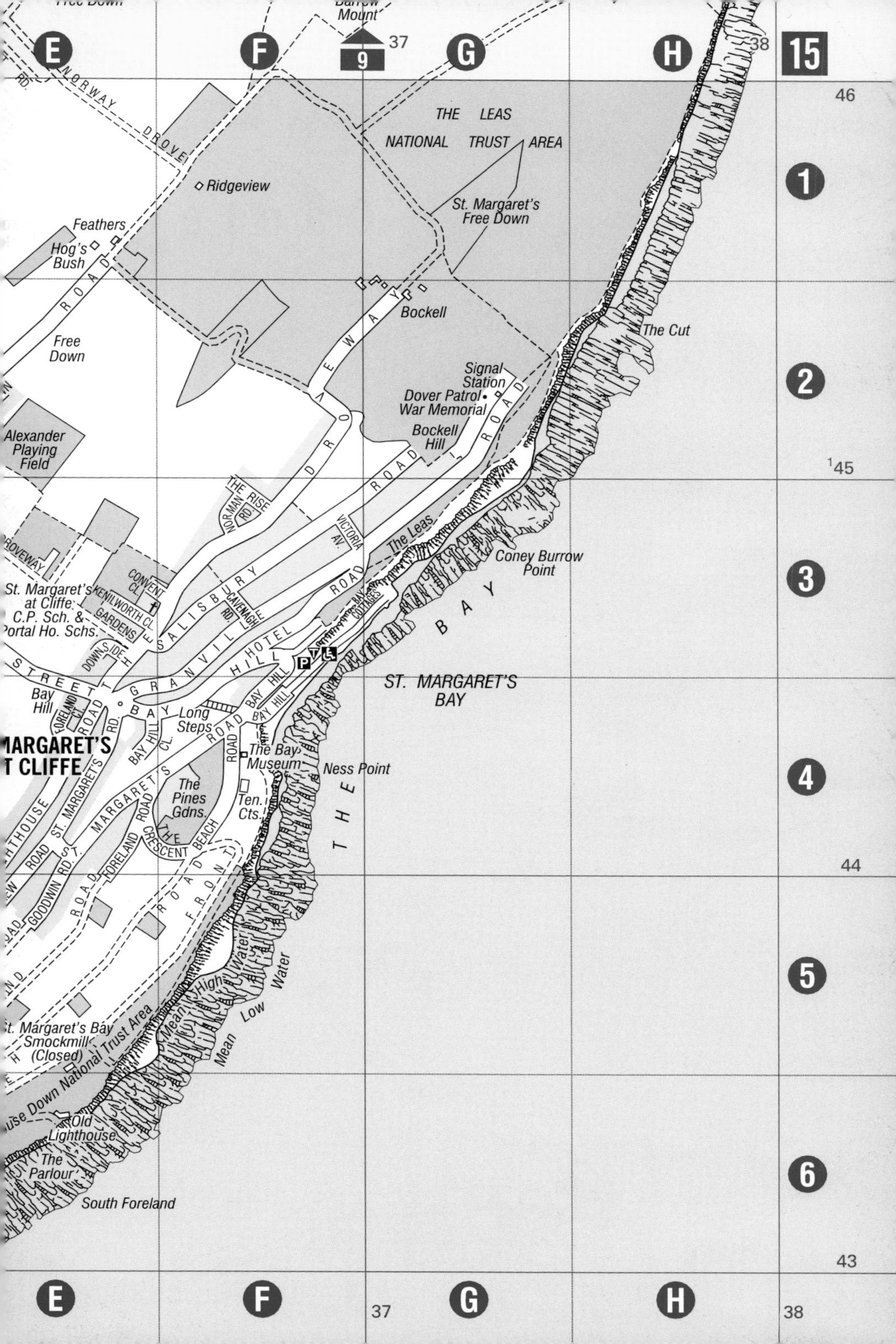

Barrow Mount
9
37
38
E
F
G
H
46
45
44
43
1
2
3
4
5
6
NORWAY DROVE
THE LEAS NATIONAL TRUST AREA
Ridgeview
St. Margaret's Free Down
Feathers
Hog's Bush
ROAD
Free Down
Bockell
DROVEWAY
The Cut
Signal Station
Dover Patrol War Memorial
Bockell Hill
ROAD
Alexander Playing Field
THE RISE
NORMAN RD.
VICTORIA AV.
The Leas
Coney Burrow Point
DROVEWAY
CONVENT CL.
KENILWORTH CL.
GARDENS
St. Margaret's at Cliffe C.P. Sch. & Portal Ho. Schs.
SALISBURY
CAVENAGH RD.
ROAD
BAY COTTAGES
BAY
HOTEL
HILL
GRANVILLE
DOWNSIDE
STREET
ST. MARGARET'S BAY
Bay Hill
FORELAND CL.
ROAD
RD.
BAY HILL CL.
Long Steps
ROAD
BAY HILL
ROAD
MARGARET'S AT CLIFFE
The Bay Museum
Ness Point
THE
ST. MARGARET'S
The Pines Gdns.
Ten. Cts.
LIGHTHOUSE
ROAD
ST. MARGARET'S RD.
FORELAND
GOODWIN
ROAD
THE CRESCENT
BEACH
THE FRONT
Mean High Water
Mean Low Water
St. Margaret's Bay Smockmill (Closed)
Lighthouse Down National Trust Area
Old Lighthouse
The Parlour
South Foreland

A
B
C
D
1
2
3
4
5
6
14
43
42
41
140
615
Rec. Grd.
CHAPEL LA.
WHITE HORSE LANE
MAGPIE LA.
Rhodes Minnis
Boyke Wood
Home Farm
Wenny Farm
Canterbur
LONGAGE
CT4
SIBTON WOOD
The Homestead
Ridge Farm
WOODLAND ROAD
Hemsted
Hill Top Farm
Great Blacklands Carvet Wood
SHEP
Longage Farm
Sibton Park Girls' Prep. Sch
Woodland
Woodland Wood
Skeete
Dingleden Wood
SKEETE ROAD
Valley Dairy Farm
BRADY ROAD
FOX CL.
ETHELBURGA GRO.
BEDINGFIELD WY.
BARTON FLD.
WOODLAND COTTS.
DOG KENNEL LA.
Valley Farm
LYMINGE
Football Grd.
Little Hollow Farm
Skeete Wood
Folke
Hempton Farm
CT18
LOUGHBOROUGH LANE
Hythe
CT21
POSTLING WOOD
Court Lodge Farm
North Downs Way
Newbarn

28

Map grid references and labels

E **F** 17
43

Tye Wood
Millhill Farm

INSET

EXTED HILL
PARK
Works
Pav.
Rec. Grd.
VALLEY
Rec. Grd.
LANE
Village Hall
FARROW

SHEPWAY

1

MILLHILL ROAD
LANE
CANTERBURY

Ottinge

Cullings Farm

Ottinge Court Farm

SHUTTLESFIELD

Lower Court

42

Mountbottom

Elham

THE BUTTS
PINE COTTS.
PROSPECT TER.
CULLINGS HILL
LING'S HILL
EAST KENT HUNT COTTS.
ST. MARY'S R.C.
HIGH ST.
CHERRY GDNS.
LIME VILLAS
BEECH VILLAS
COCK
DUCK ST.
Water Farm
WATER FARM

144

2

East Kent Hunt Kennels
VICARAGE
NEW ROAD
OLD ROAD
LA
ORCHARDS
Rec. Grd.
HUG GREEN
THE HALT

Elham C. of E. Prim. Sch.
Cemetery

Collards Wood

Canterbury

COLLARDS LANE

CANTERBURY

Nail Bourne

CT4

3

The Laynes

Nail Bourne
Bourne

A **Y**

Yewtree Cross

Little Stonebridge

Great Shuttlesfield Farm

18

4

Shuttlesfield

CANTERBURY ROAD
CANTERBURY ROAD
MUSS. R.
ROBUS CL.
THE WOODIES
NORTH LYMINGE
TYE SIDINGS

Little Shuttlesfield Farm
41

18

Nail LA.

North Lyminge

KIMBERLEY TER.
WESLEY TER.
Lyminge C. of E. Prim. Sch.
Tayne Fld.
NASH HILL
Library

Red House Farm

5

MAYFIELD RD.
WENTWTH. CL.
JOHNSONWDS.
RECTORY LA.
WELL RD.
CHURCH ROAD
STATION RD.
GREENBANKS
ECHURST CL.
Hall

Eastcourt

STREET END
East

o **n** **e**

Broad Street

ETCHINGHILL GOLF COURSE

Brook

Sunningdale Farm

6

Teddars Leas House

140

Club House

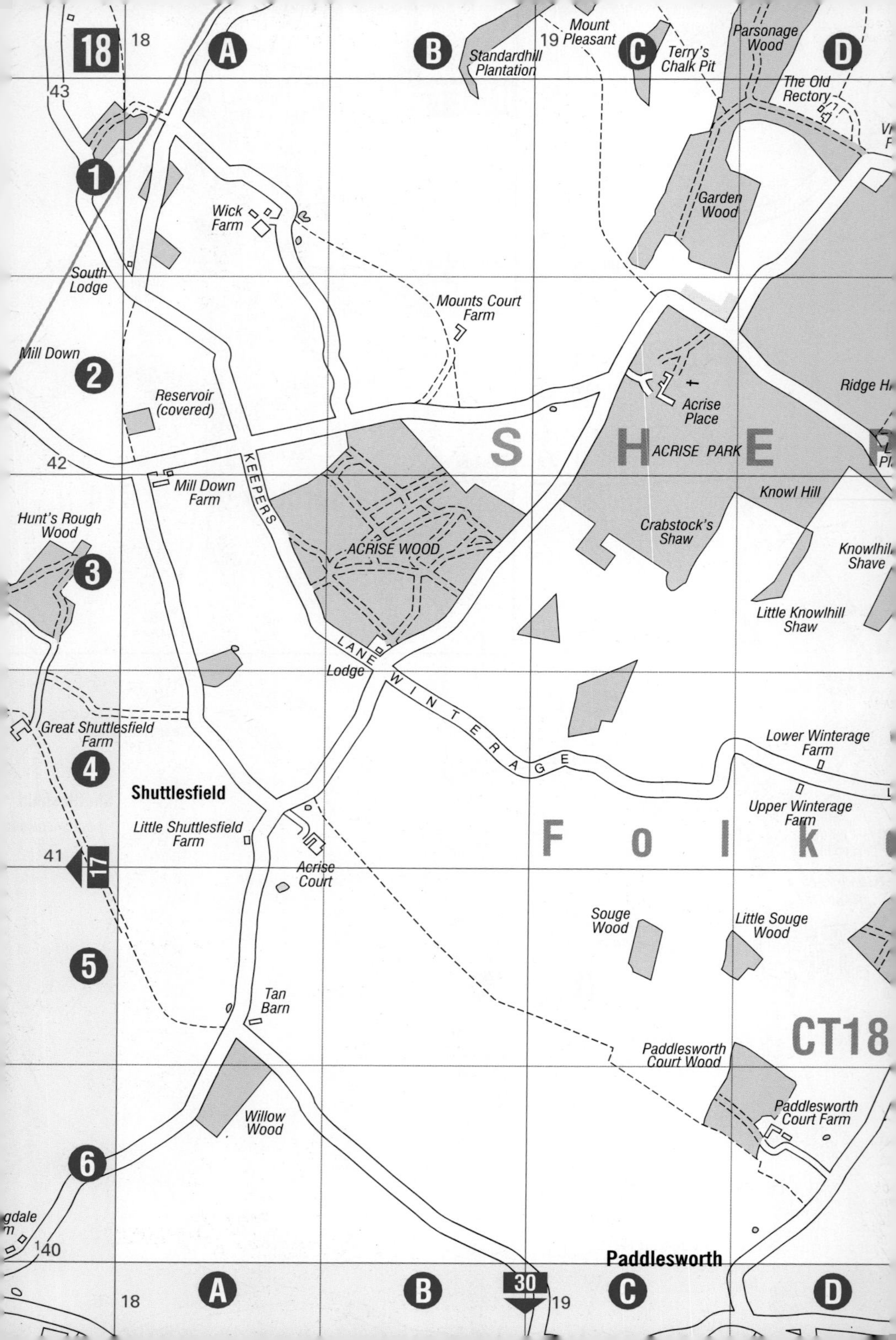
18
18
A
B
C
D
19
Mount Pleasant
Standardhill Plantation
Terry's Chalk Pit
Parsonage Wood
The Old Rectory
43
1
Wick Farm
Garden Wood
South Lodge
Mounts Court Farm
Mill Down
2
Reservoir (covered)
Acrise Place
Ridge H
S
H
E
ACRISE PARK
42
Mill Down Farm
KEEPERS
Knowl Hill
Hunt's Rough Wood
Crabstock's Shaw
3
ACRISE WOOD
Knowlhil Shave
Little Knowlhill Shaw
LANE
Lodge
WINTERAGE
Great Shuttlesfield Farm
Lower Winterage Farm
4
Shuttlesfield
Upper Winterage Farm
Little Shuttlesfield Farm
F
o
l
k
41
17
Acrise Court
Souge Wood
Little Souge Wood
5
Tan Barn
CT18
Paddlesworth Court Wood
Willow Wood
Paddlesworth Court Farm
6
gdale
m
140
Paddlesworth
A
B
30
C
D
18
19

Hoad Farm
Butterfly Cen.
Frogshall Cotts.
Garden House
Clevelands
The Homestead
Cold Blows
Pinecote
Belmont
Dover
CT15
Longcraft Wood
Chipdene
Minnis House
Meadow View
FOX HOLT ROAD
Foxholt Cottage
Thorndean
Little Foxholt
Minnis Beech
Ridge Hill Plantation
The Mead Cottage
Acorn Cottage
Rosendale
Caroline Cottage
Red House Farm
Pound Farm
Ridge Farm
Ridge Row
CANTERBURY ROAD
A260
Little Densole Farm
Whitegate Plantation
DENSOLE LA.
Densole Farm
BLACK HORSE FARM CARAVAN & CAMPING PARK
DENSOLE WAY
Mayfield Farm
White Gates
COACH ROAD
DENSOLE
REINDEN WOOD
SCHOOL ROAD
ST. JOHN'S CL.
ST. JOHN'S WY.
PAY STREET
Bush Farm
Woodside
MINTER CL.
NURSERY LA.
Limes Farm Equestrian Cen.
NURSERY CL.
AVENUE
Reinden Wood House
Roods Meadow Farm
Lavender
Fernfield Farm
Cricket Ground
Pav.
Cobham's Rough
Sweet Briar
The Cabin
Whitepost Wood
Pay Street Farm
Milgate Farm
CRICKETERS CL.
FERN CL.
MILLFIELD
COWGATE
OAK DR.
Mill House
Cemetery
Crematorium
BARNHURST LANE
ST. DENYS RD.
HAWKINGE
AERODROME ROAD
Hawkinge C. P. Sch.
Sewage Works
CEMETERY COTTAGES
GILLMAN CL.
MEGONE
DRIVE
GREBE CL.
HART CL.
E
F
G
H
1
2
3
4
5
6
21
22
43
42
41
40
20
31

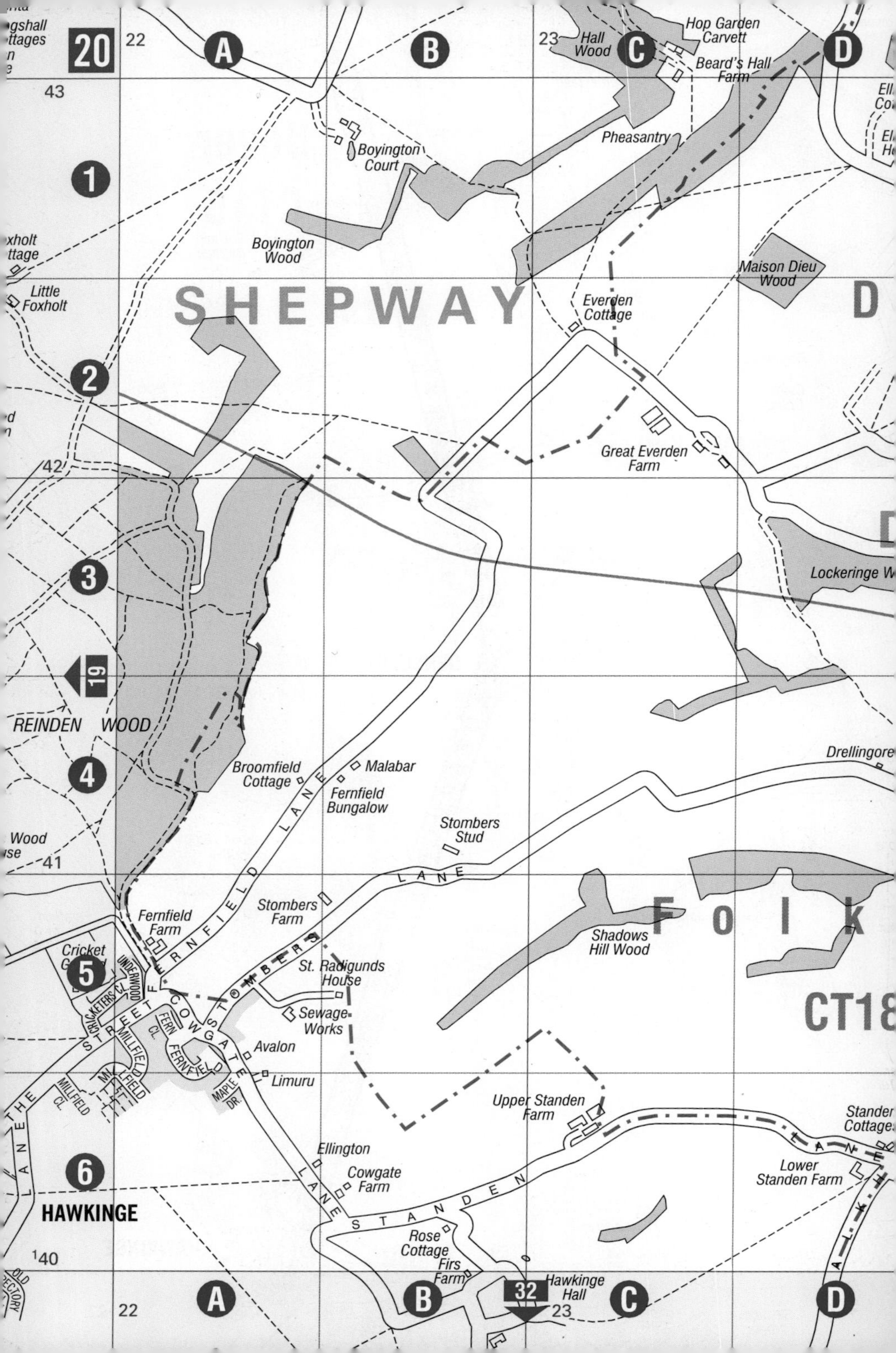
SHEPWAY
Hall Wood
Hop Garden Carvett
Beard's Hall Farm
Boyington Court
Pheasantry
Boyington Wood
Maison Dieu Wood
Little Foxholt
Everden Cottage
Great Everden Farm
Lockeringe W
REINDEN WOOD
Broomfield Cottage
Malabar
Fernfield Bungalow
Drellingore
Stombers Stud
FERNFIELD LANE
STOMBERS LANE
Stombers Farm
Fernfield Farm
Shadows Hill Wood
Folk
CT18
Cricket Ground
UNDERWOOD
CRICKETERS CL.
STREET
COWGATE
St. Radigunds House
Sewage Works
FERN CL.
FERNFIELD
MILLFIELD
Avalon
Limuru
MAPLE DR.
MILLFIELD CL.
THE LANE
Upper Standen Farm
Standen Cottages
Lower Standen Farm
Ellington
Cowgate Farm
COWGATE LANE
STANDEN LANE
HAWKINGE
Rose Cottage
Firs Farm
Hawkinge Hall
OLD RECTORY
19
32
A
B
C
D
1
2
3
4
5
6
22
23
43
42
41
40

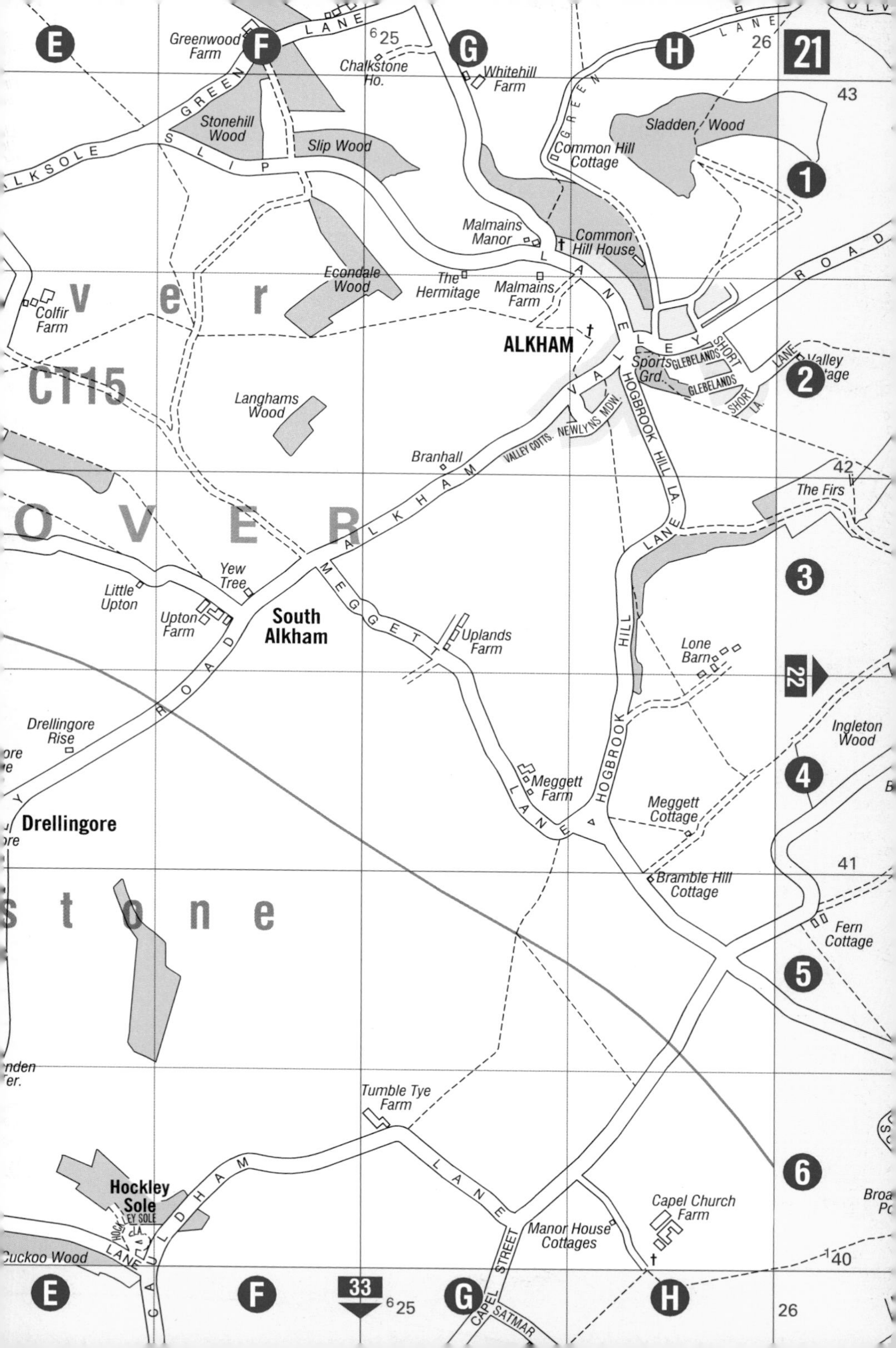
Greenwood Farm
Chalkstone Ho.
Whitehill Farm
Stonehill Wood
Slip Wood
Sladden Wood
Common Hill Cottage
Malmains Manor
Common Hill House
Econdale Wood
The Hermitage
Malmains Farm
Colfir Farm
ALKHAM
Sports Grd.
GLEBELANDS
SHORT LA.
Valley Cottage
CT15
Langhams Wood
Branhall
VALLEY COTTS.
NEWLYNS MDW.
HOGBROOK HILL LA.
The Firs
DOVER
Yew Tree
Little Upton
Upton Farm
South Alkham
MEGGETT LANE
Uplands Farm
Lone Barn
Ingleton Wood
Drellingore Rise
Drellingore
Meggett Farm
Meggett Cottage
Bramble Hill Cottage
Fern Cottage
Folkestone
Tumble Tye Farm
Hockley Sole
ALKHAM ROAD
ALKHAM VALLEY ROAD
Capel Church Farm
Manor House Cottages
Cuckoo Wood
CAPEL STREET
SATMAR
CAULDHAM LANE
E F G H
1 2 3 4 5 6
22
33

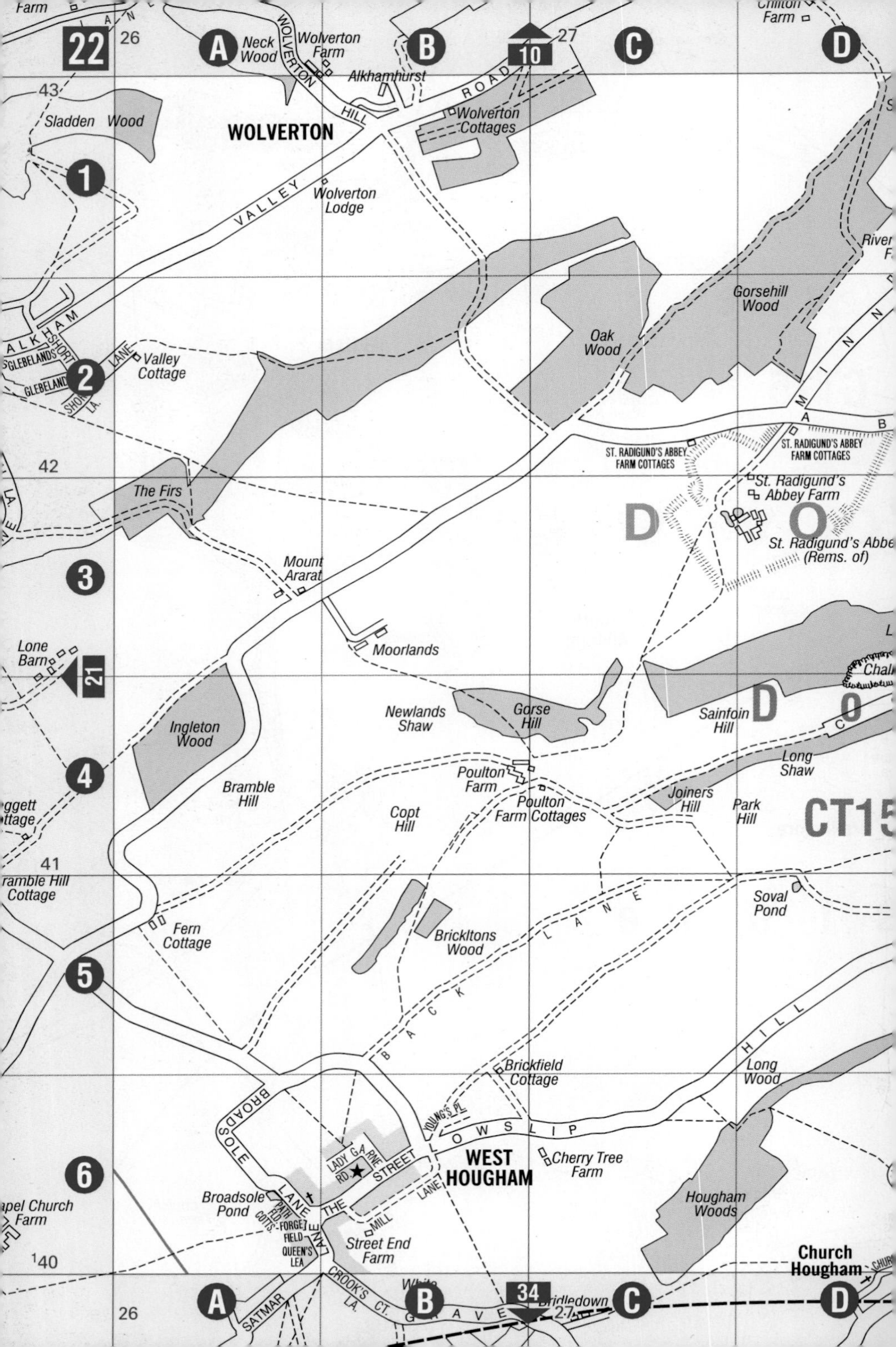
22
A
B
C
D
10
26
27
Neck Wood
Wolverton Farm
Alkhamhurst
Chilton Farm
WOLVERTON
Sladden Wood
Wolverton Cottages
WOLVERTON HILL
VALLEY ROAD
Wolverton Lodge
River
Gorsehill Wood
Oak Wood
ALKHAM
SHORT LANE
GLEBELANDS
Valley Cottage
A 2
St. Radigund's Abbey Farm Cottages
St. Radigund's Abbey Farm
St. Radigund's Abbey (Rems. of)
The Firs
Mount Ararat
Moorlands
Lone Barn
21
Newlands Shaw
Gorse Hill
Sainfoin Hill
Ingleton Wood
Bramble Hill
Poulton Farm
Poulton Farm Cottages
Joiners Hill
Park Hill
Long Shaw
Copt Hill
CT15
Bramble Hill Cottage
Soval Pond
Fern Cottage
Brickltons Wood
BACK LANE
Brickfield Cottage
Long Wood
HILL
BROADSOLE LANE
YOUNG'S PL.
LOWSLIP
WEST HOUGHAM
Cherry Tree Farm
LADY GARNE RD.
THE STREET
MILL LANE
Broadsole Pond
Hougham Woods
FORGE FIELD
QUEEN'S LEA
Street End Farm
Church Hougham
CROOK'S CT.
SATMAR LA.
GRAVE
Bridledown
34
1
2
3
4
5
6
43
42
41
140

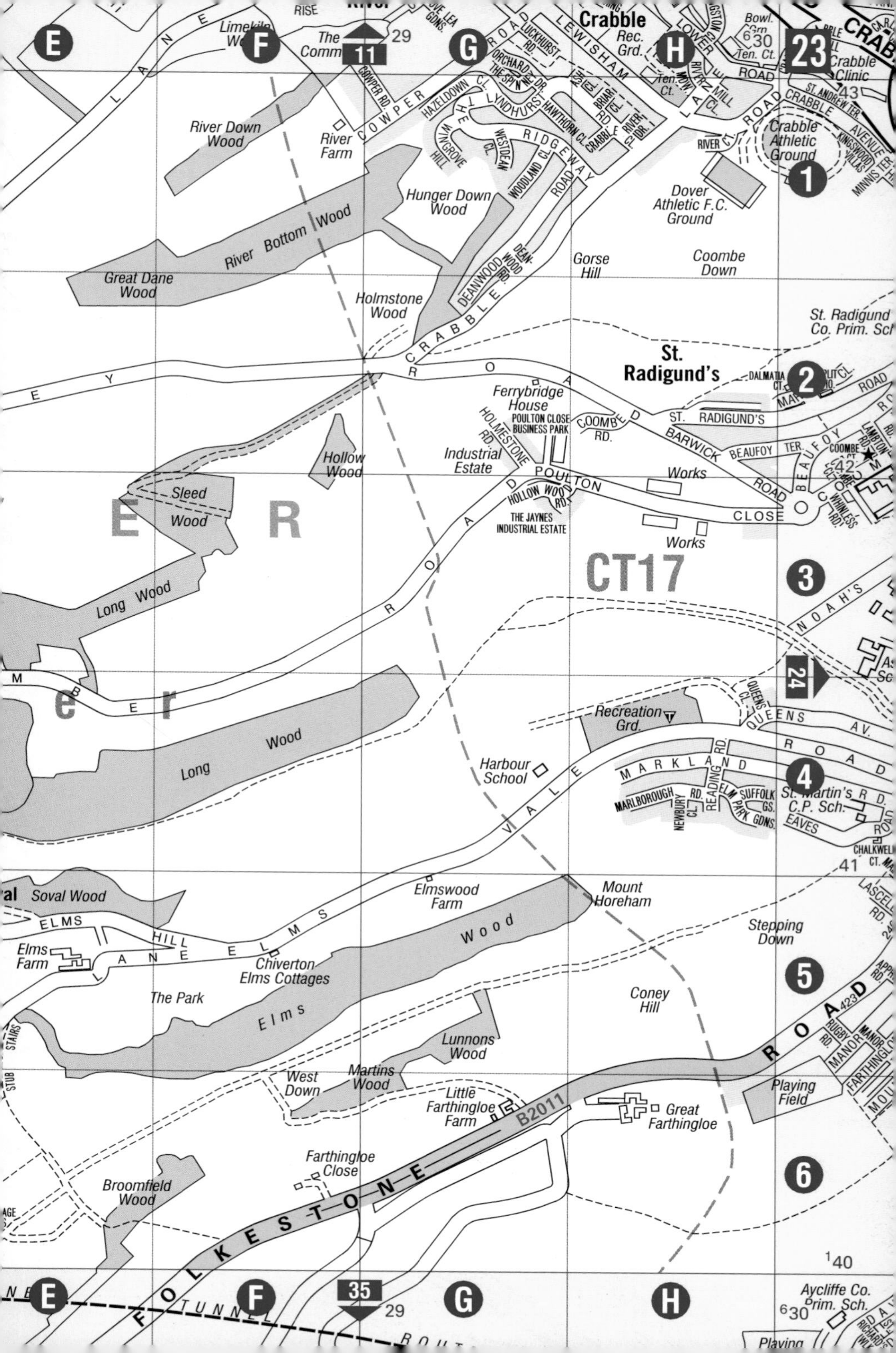
E
F
G
H
23
11
35
24
29
630
Crabble
Rec. Grd.
The Comm
Limekiln Wood
River Down Wood
River Farm
Hunger Down Wood
River Bottom Wood
Great Dane Wood
Holmstone Wood
Gorse Hill
Coombe Down
Dover Athletic F.C. Ground
Crabble Athletic Ground
Crabble Clinic
St. Radigund's
St. Radigund Co. Prim. Sch
Ferrybridge House
Poulton Close Business Park
Industrial Estate
The Jaynes Industrial Estate
Works
Hollow Wood
Sleed Wood
Long Wood
CT17
Recreation Grd.
Harbour School
St. Martin's C.P. Sch.
Elmswood Farm
Mount Horeham
Stepping Down
Soval Wood
Elms Farm
Chiverton Elms Cottages
The Park
Elms Wood
Coney Hill
Lunnons Wood
West Down
Martins Wood
Little Farthingloe Farm
Great Farthingloe
Farthingloe Close
Broomfield Wood
Playing Field
Aycliffe Co. Prim. Sch.
Folkestone Road
B2011
Crabble Road
Poulton Close
Barwick Road
Coombe Rd.
Holmestone Rd.
Hollow Wood Rd.
Ridgeway
Cowper Road
Lewisham Road
Markland Road
Queens Av.
Elms Vale
Elms Hill
Elms Lane
Noah's
1
2
3
4
5
6
43
42
41
140

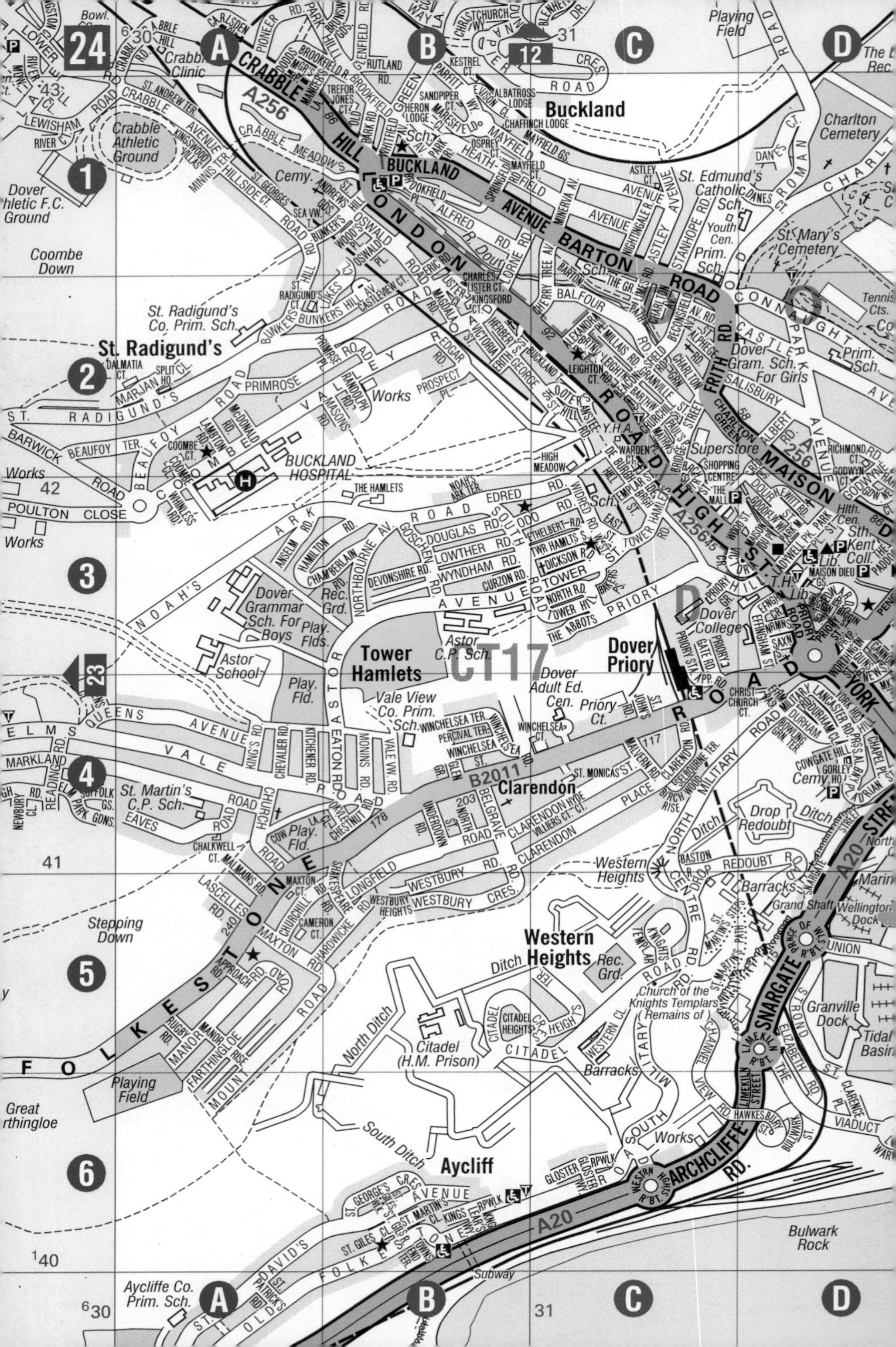

24
Buckland
St. Radigund's
Tower Hamlets
CT17
Dover Priory
Clarendon
Western Heights
Aycliff
Citadel (H.M. Prison)
Buckland Hospital
Dover Grammar Sch. For Boys
Astor School
Charlton Cemetery
St. Mary's Cemetery
Dover College
Coombe Down
Stepping Down
Dover Athletic F.C. Ground
Crabble Athletic Ground
Bulwark Rock
Granville Dock
Folkestone Road
London Road
High St.
Archcliffe Rd.
Snargate
A256
A20
B2011
12
23

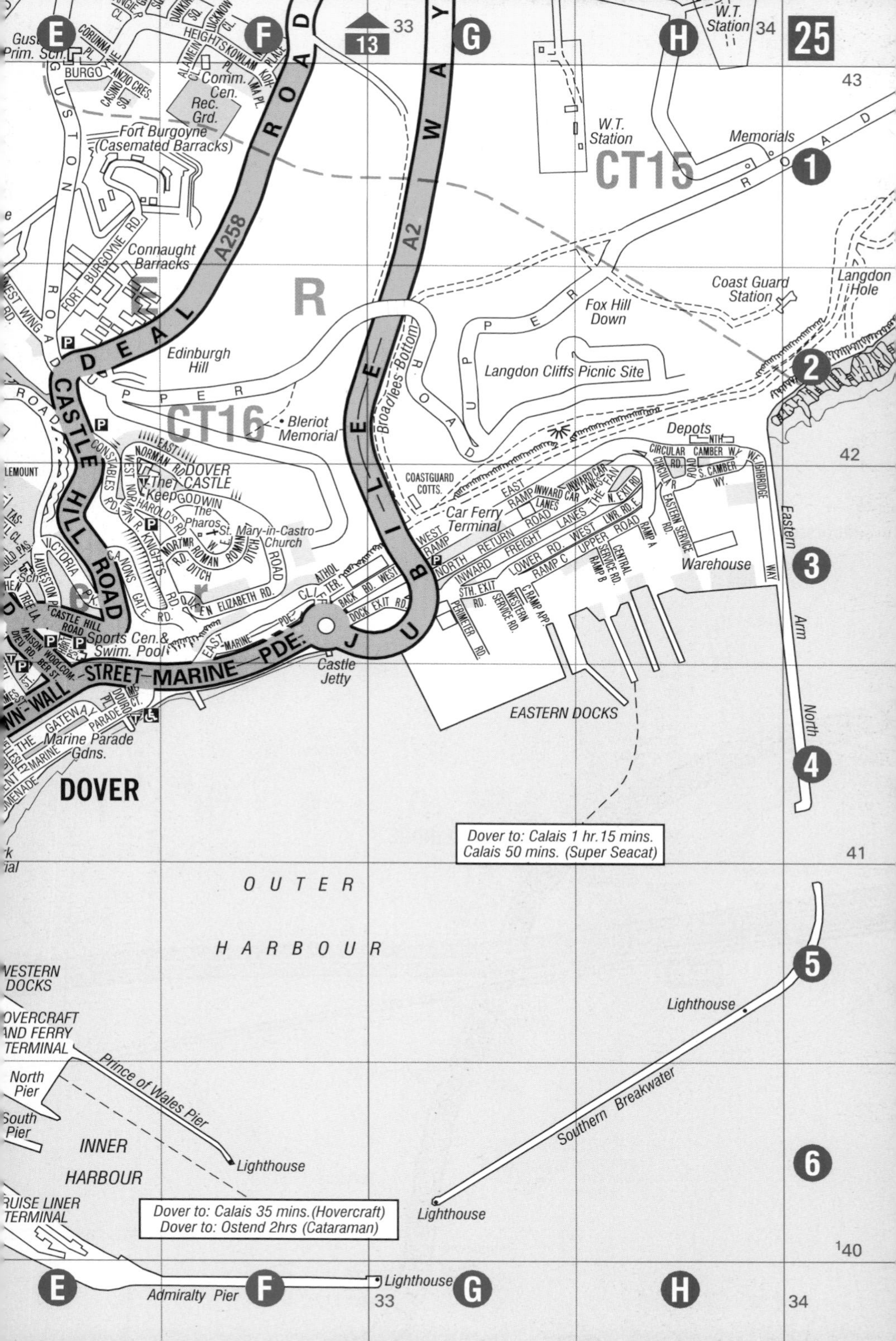

Gust.
Prim. Sch.
E

F

13 33

G

H W.T. Station 34

CORUNNA
PL.

HEIGHTS
ALAMEIN
KOWLN
PL.
Comm.
Cen.
Rec.
Grd.

BURGO

ANDU CRES.

Fort Burgoyne
(Casemated Barracks)

W.T.
Station

CT15

Memorials **1**

Connaught
Barracks

GUSTON ROAD

DEAL ROAD

A258

A2

Coast Guard
Station

Langdon
Hole

WEST WING RD.

FORT BURGOYNE RD.

Edinburgh
Hill

P

Fox Hill
Down

Langdon Cliffs Picnic Site

2

CT16

Bleriot
Memorial

Broadlees Bottom

Langdon Cliffs Picnic Site

42

P

D E A L

P

E

R

U

P

P

E

R

E

L

E

E

R O A D

Depots

NTH
CAMBER WY.
S. CAMBER
WY.

CIRCULAR
RD.

Warehouse

Eastern

North

3

4

CASTLE HILL ROAD

NORMAN
The
Keep
GODWIN
The Pharos
St. Mary-in-Castro
Church

DOVER CASTLE

COASTGUARD
COTTS.

Car Ferry
Terminal

EAST
INWARD CAR
LANES

INWARD
FREIGHT RD.

CAMBER RD.

EASTERN SERVICE RD.

WEST
RAMP
NORTH

EAST
RAMP
INWARD RD.

THE TAIL

EXIT RD.

RAMP A

ROAD

VICTORIA

CASTLE HILL ROAD

P

Sports Cen.&
Swim. Pool

WEST RETURN ROAD

LOWER RD. WEST

LWR. RD.

UPPER ROAD

RAMP B

CENTRAL SERVICE RD.

SERVICE RD.

RAMP C

STH. EXIT
RD.

STAMP APP.

ST. MARINE

ST.

QUEEN ELIZABETH RD.

CLIFTER.

CATHOL

BACK RD. WEST

DOCK EXIT RD.

WEST
RD.

SERVICE RD.

PERIMETER RD.

STREET MARINE PDE.

Castle
Jetty

DOVER

Marine Parade
Gdns.

MARINE PDE.

EAST

JUB

EASTERN DOCKS

Dover to: Calais 1 hr. 15 mins.
Calais 50 mins. (Super Seacat)

41

OUTER

HARBOUR

5

WESTERN
DOCKS

HOVERCRAFT
AND FERRY
TERMINAL

North
Pier

Prince of Wales Pier

Lighthouse

Southern Breakwater

South
Pier

INNER

HARBOUR

Lighthouse

6

CRUISE LINER
TERMINAL

Lighthouse

Dover to: Calais 35 mins. (Hovercraft)
Dover to: Ostend 2hrs (Cataraman)

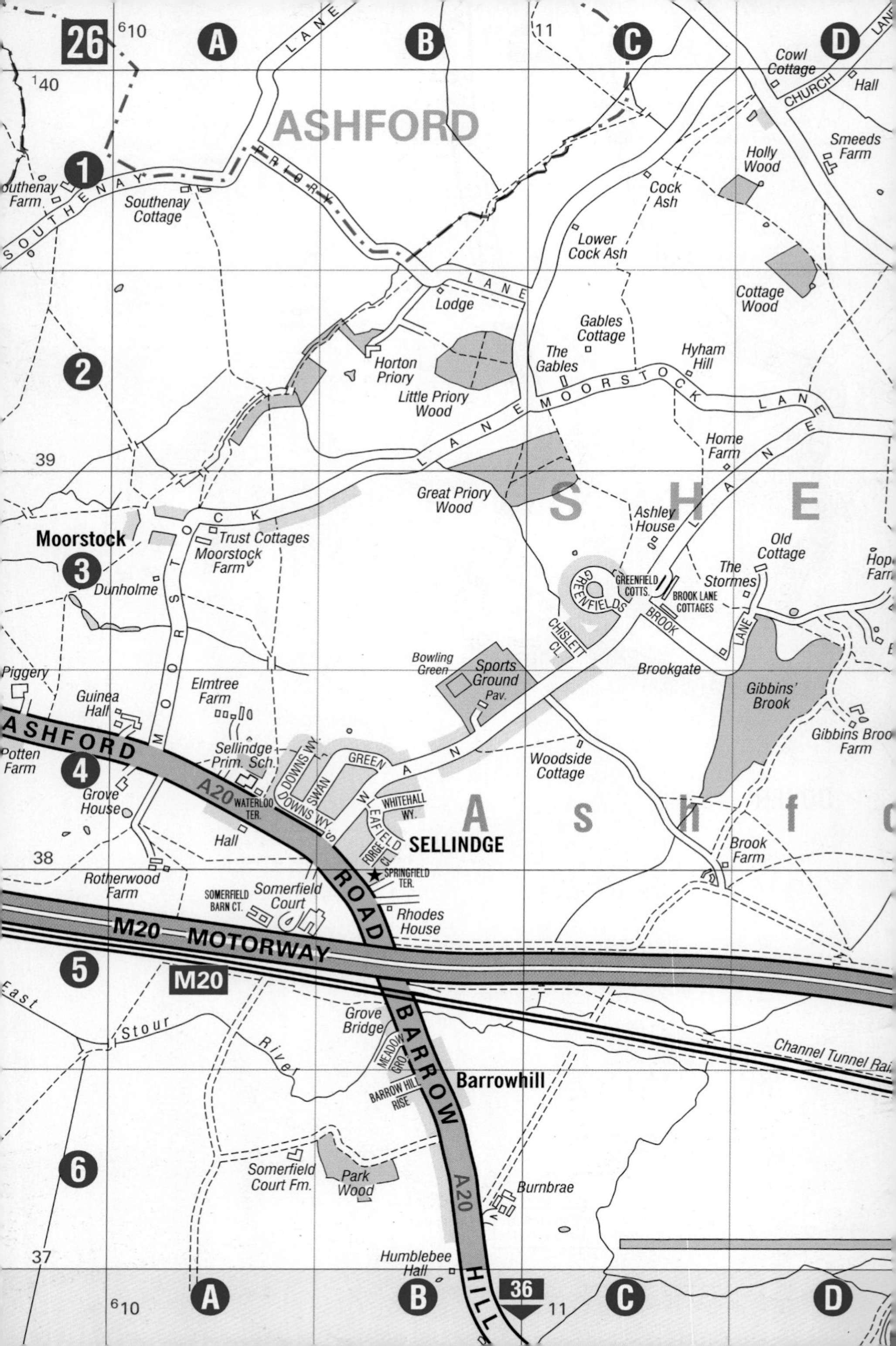

ASHFORD
Southenay Farm
Southenay Cottage
SOUTHENAY
PRIORY
LANE
Cock Ash
Lower Cock Ash
Cowl Cottage
CHURCH
Hall
Smeeds Farm
Holly Wood
Cottage Wood
Lodge
Horton Priory
Little Priory Wood
Gables Cottage
The Gables
Hyham Hill
MOORSTOCK LANE
Home Farm
Great Priory Wood
SHEPWAY
Moorstock
Trust Cottages
Moorstock Farm
Dunholme
Ashley House
Old Cottage
The Stormes
GREENFIELDS
GREENFIELD COTTS.
BROOK LANE COTTAGES
BROOK LANE
CHISLETT CL.
Bowling Green
Sports Ground
Pav.
Brookgate
Gibbins' Brook
Gibbins Brook Farm
Piggery
Guinea Hall
Elmtree Farm
ASHFORD ROAD
Potten Farm
Sellindge Prim. Sch.
DOWNS WY.
SWAN
GREEN
Woodside Cottage
A20
WATERLOO TER.
WHITEHALL WY.
LEAFIELD
FORGE CL.
Grove House
Hall
SELLINDGE
Ashford
Brook Farm
SPRINGFIELD TER.
Rotherwood Farm
SOMERFIELD BARN CT.
Somerfield Court
Rhodes House
M20 MOTORWAY
M20
East Stour River
Grove Bridge
MEADOW GRO.
BARROW HILL
Channel Tunnel Rail
Barrowhill
BARROW HILL RISE
Somerfield Court Fm.
Park Wood
Burnbrae
Humblebee Hall
36

E
F
G
H
13
14
HEMPTON HILL
North Downs Way
140
The Outlook
Monks Horton Manor
Lodge
Pilgrims' Way
Brickclamp Wood
STONE STREET
B2068
LANE
Pent Lodge
The Pent
BLINDHOUSE LANE
Blindhouse
Hayton Wood
Coppice Wood
39
Court F
WAY
Hythe
Hayton Manor Farm
Hayton Manor
ROAD
HAYTON ROAD
28
CHURCH FIELD
Waverley
CT21
Stanford
Yew Tree Farm
YEW TREE CL.
School House
The Old Rectory
Butcher Wood
38
Kennet House
KENNET LANE
Kennet La. Cotts.
The Old Mill
TN25
BECKLEY PL.
Holmdene
M20
M20 MOTORWAY
Junction 11
Perry Wood
Fairmead Farm
Completion Late 2002)
Westenhanger
STONE ST.
Westenhanger
Grand Stands
STREET
Honeywood Plantation
Honeywood Cottages
A20
ASHFORD RD
Hillhurst Farm
Lodge
37
FOLKESTONE RACE COURSE
STONE
37
13
14

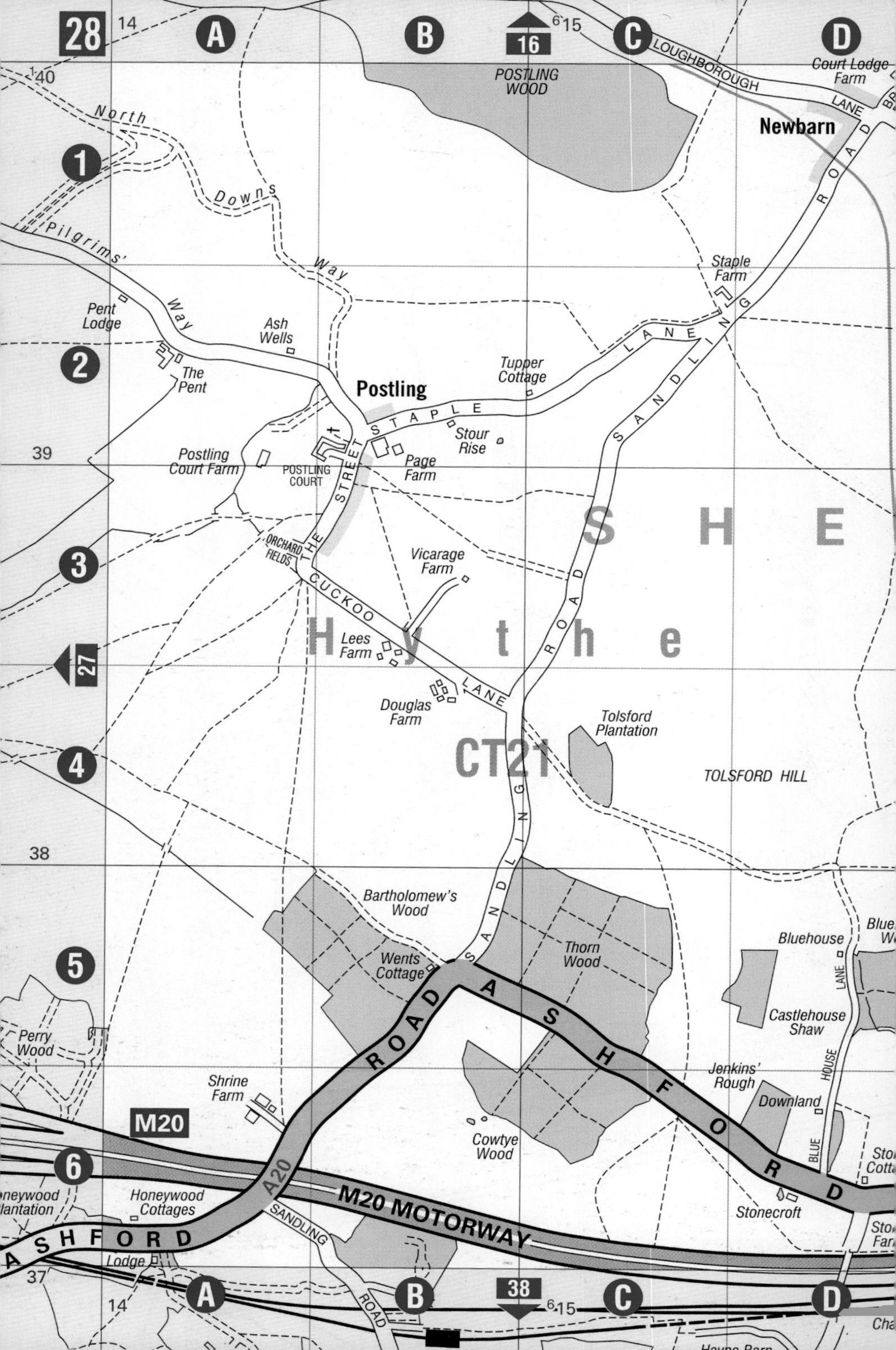
A
B
16
C
D
Postling Wood
Loughborough Lane
Court Lodge Farm
Newbarn
North Downs Way
Pilgrims' Way
Pent Lodge
Ash Wells
The Pent
Staple Farm
Tupper Cottage
Postling
Staple Lane
Stour Rise
Postling Court Farm
Postling Court
Page Farm
The Street
Orchard Fields
Sandling Road
Vicarage Farm
Cuckoo Lane
Hythe
Lees Farm
Douglas Farm
Tolsford Plantation
CT21
Tolsford Hill
Bartholomew's Wood
Thorn Wood
Wents Cottage
Bluehouse
Bluehouse Lane
Castlehouse Shaw
Ashford Road
Perry Wood
Jenkins' Rough
Shrine Farm
Downland
M20
Cowtye Wood
A20
M20 Motorway
Honeywood Cottages
Stonecroft
Sandling Road
Lodge
Hayne Barn
38
27
1
2
3
4
5
6
39
38
37
14
6 15

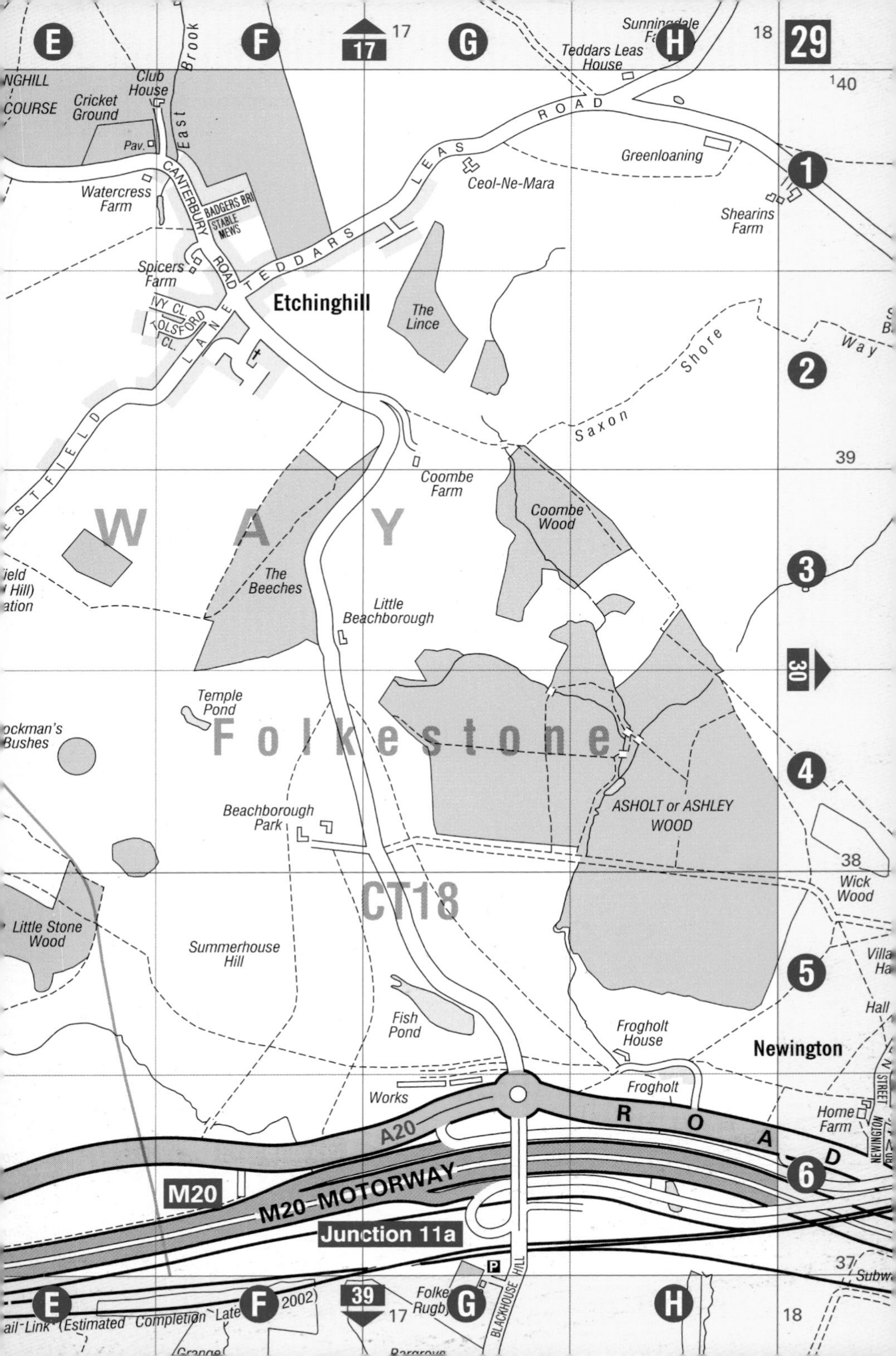

E
F
G
H
17
18
1
2
3
4
5
6
30
39
37
38
40
Etchinghill
Newington
Folkestone
CT18
WAY
Sunningdale
Teddars Leas House
TEDDARS LEAS ROAD
Greenloaning
Ceol-Ne-Mara
Shearins Farm
Club House
Cricket Ground
Pav.
East Brook
Watercress Farm
CANTERBURY ROAD
BADGERS BRI
STABLE MEWS
Spicers Farm
IVY CL.
TOLSFORD CL.
LANE
The Lince
Saxon Shore Way
Coombe Farm
Coombe Wood
The Beeches
Little Beachborough
Temple Pond
Beachborough Park
ASHOLT or ASHLEY WOOD
Wick Wood
Little Stone Wood
Summerhouse Hill
Fish Pond
Frogholt House
Frogholt
Works
A20
ROAD
M20
M20-MOTORWAY
Junction 11a
Home Farm
NEWINGTON STREET
BLACKHOUSE HILL
Hall
Rugby
2002)
Completion
Estimated

A
B
C
D
18
19
18
Paddlesworth
Shearins Farm
Cole Farm
Sole Farm
Shearins Bungalow
Saxon Shore Way
North Downs Way
Home Farm
Arpinge
Parsonage Farm
Stonehill Bank Shave
Lower Arpinge Farm
Arpinge House
Arpinge Wood
Pigeonhouse Wood
Hungar Down
Upper Arpinge Farm
Upper Arpinge House
29
Chalk Pit Kilns
Northcliffe
Cherito Hill
PEENE COTTAGES
Peene
DANTON LANE
Wick Wood
UNDERHILL COTTS.
HILL ROAD
Peene Farm
CHANNEL TUNNEL RAIL TERMINAL
Elham Valley Railway Museum
Village Hall
French Border Controls
Hall
U.K. Border Controls
U.K. Terminal
Newington
Customs
French Border Controls
Pound Farm
U.K. Border Controls
NEWINGTON
THE STREET
Home Farm
SCHOOL LA.
Newington Grange
NEWINGTON RD
Tolls
ASHFORD ROAD
Junction 12
LONGPORT ROAD
A20
M20
M20 MOTORWAY
A20
Subway
CHERITON HIGH STREET
40
Superstore
Superstore
Eurotunnel Customer Service Centre
ROMAN WAY
SAMIAN CR.
TIBER CL.
FIRS CLOSE
LANGDON RD.
WOOD CTGE LA.
STAR LA.
MORSE CT.
SHAFTES
CHERITON WD. HO.
MITCHELL
WEYMOUTH
RICHMOND ST.
S H E
F o l k
CT1
1
2
3
4
5
6
39
38
37

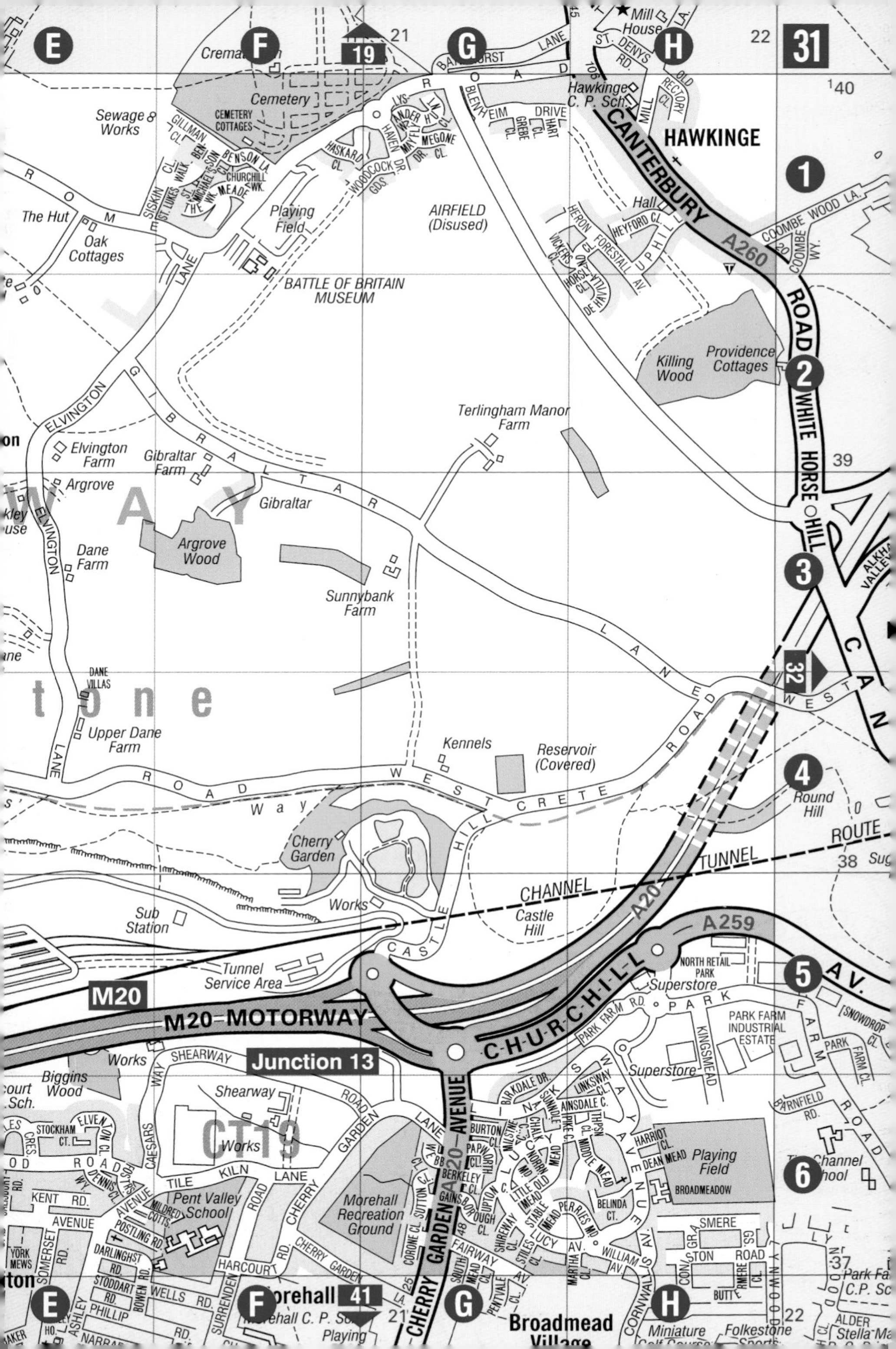

31
E
F
G
H
19
21
22
Mill House
Crematorium
Cemetery
CEMETERY COTTAGES
Sewage Works
BARHURST LANE
ST. DENYS RD.
OLD RECTORY CL.
MILL LA.
Hawkinge C. P. Sch.
BLENHEIM DRIVE
GREBE CL.
HART CL.
HAWKINGE
CANTERBURY
A260
ROAD
WHITE HORSE HILL
140
1
2
3
4
5
6
39
38
37
GILLMAN CL.
BENSON LA.
CHURCHILL WK.
THE MEADE
SISKIN CL.
ST. LUKES WALK
HASKARD CL.
WOODCOCK GDS.
MAYFLY DR.
MEGONE CL.
The Hut
Oak Cottages
Playing Field
AIRFIELD (Disused)
BATTLE OF BRITAIN MUSEUM
HERON FORESTALL
HEYFORD CL.
VICKERS CL.
HORSLEY CL.
DE HAVILLAND
UPHILL
Hall
COOMBE WOOD LA.
COOMBE WY.
Killing Wood
Providence Cottages
ELVINGTON LANE
Elvington Farm
Gibraltar Farm
Argrove
GIBRALTAR LANE
Terlingham Manor Farm
Gibraltar
Argrove Wood
Dane Farm
Sunnybank Farm
DANE VILLAS
Upper Dane Farm
ALKHAM VALLEY
32
WEST
CAN
Kennels
Reservoir (Covered)
ROAD WEST CRETE ROAD
Way
Round Hill
ROUTE
TUNNEL
CHANNEL
Cherry Garden
HILL
CASTLE HILL
Castle Hill
Works
Sub Station
A20
A259
Tunnel Service Area
NORTH RETAIL PARK
Superstore
M20
M20 MOTORWAY
Junction 13
CHURCHILL AV.
PARK FARM RD.
PARK FARM INDUSTRIAL ESTATE
KINGSMEAD
SNOWDROP CL.
PARK FARM CL.
Works
Biggins Wood
SHEARWAY
Shearway
CT19
CAESARS WAY
Works
CHERRY GARDEN LANE
CHERRY GARDEN AVENUE
A20
BIRKDALE DR.
LINKSWAY
SUNNINGDALE
AINSDALE C.
HARRIOT CL.
DEAN MEAD
Playing Field
BROADMEADOW
BARNFIELD RD.
FARM ROAD
The Channel School
STOCKHAM CT.
ELVENTON CL.
TILE KILN LANE
Pent Valley School
MILDRED COTTS.
POSTLING RD.
DARLINGHST RD.
STODDART RD.
PHILLIP
KENT RD.
AVENUE
YORK MEWS
SOMERSET RD.
HARCOURT
WELLS RD.
SURRENDEN
Morehall Recreation Ground
CHERRY GARDEN
BURTON CL.
PAPWORTH CL.
BERKELEY CL.
GAINSBOROUGH CL.
SUTTON CL.
CORONE CL.
FAIRWAY
SOUTHMEAD CL.
PENTVALE CL.
SHIREWAY CL.
STILES CL.
LUCY AV.
PERRIES MD.
WILLIAM AV.
BELINDA CT.
CORNWALLIS AV.
CONISTON ROAD
BUTTERMERE CL.
Morehall
41
Morehall C. P. Sch.
Broadmead Village
Miniature Golf Course
Folkestone Sports
Park Farm C.P. Sch.
ALDER

32
HAWKINGE
Hawkinge Hall
Flegis Court
Coombe Wood
Providence Cottages
Killing Wood
Havenfield Lodge
Encliffe Farm
Hillside Farm
Hithervale Farm
Thorneybank
Long Meadow
Havenfield Hall
Lady Wood
Coombe Farm
Lady Wood Bungalow
Sunnybank Farm
Khimera Farm
SHEPWAY
Palmer's Hill
Hope Farm
Yon Farm
Folkes
Round Hill
Sugarloaf Hill
Creteway Down
CT19
Wingate Hill
North Retail Park
Park Farm Industrial Estate
The Channel School
Playing Field
Park Farm C.P. Sch.
George Spurgen C.P. Sch.
Works
CANTERBURY RD.
WHITE HORSE HILL
A260
A20
ALKHAM VALLEY RD.
CANTERBURY
CHURCHILL AVENUE
A259
HILL
DOVER ROAD
B2011
CHANNEL
North Downs Way
20
31
42

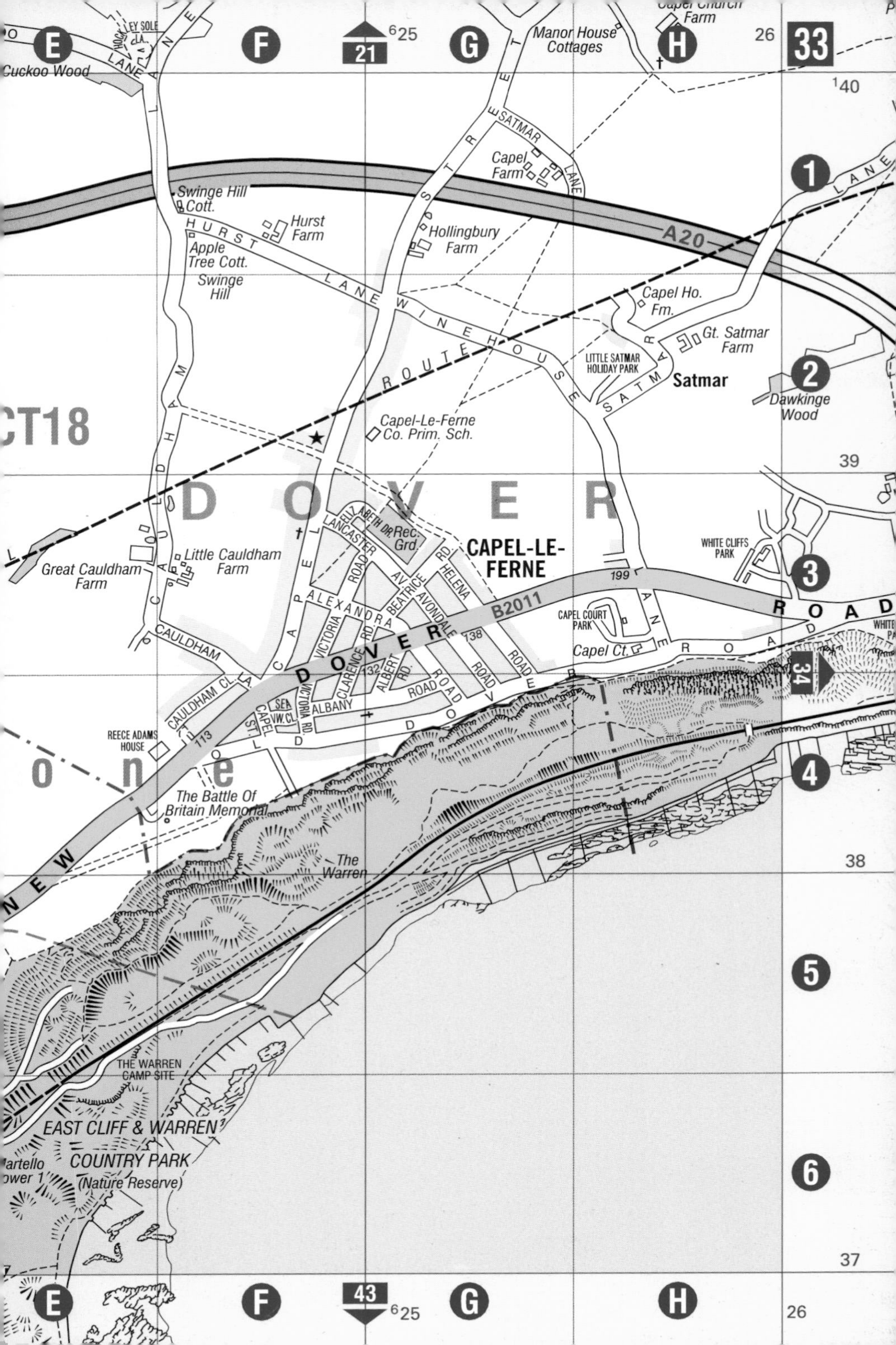

E
F
G
H
21
43
34
CT18
DOVER
Capel Church Farm
Manor House Cottages
Cuckoo Wood
LEY SOLE LA.
HOCK
LANE
Swinge Hill Cott.
Hurst Farm
HURST LANE
Apple Tree Cott.
Swinge Hill
SATMAR LANE
Capel Farm
Hollingbury Farm
STREET
A20
Capel Ho. Fm.
Gt. Satmar Farm
LITTLE SATMAR HOLIDAY PARK
Satmar
Dawkinge Wood
WINEHOUSE LANE
ROUTE
Capel-Le-Ferne Co. Prim. Sch.
CAULDHAM LANE
Great Cauldham Farm
Little Cauldham Farm
ELIZABETH DR.
Rec. Grd.
LANCASTER ROAD
CAPEL-LE-FERNE
WHITE CLIFFS PARK
HELENA RD.
B2011
ALEXANDRA RD.
BEATRICE AV.
AVONDALE
CAPEL COURT PARK
Capel Ct.
ROAD
DOVER ROAD
VICTORIA RD.
CLARENCE RD.
ALBERT RD.
CAULDHAM
CAULDHAM CL.
CAPEL ST.
SEA VW. CL.
ALBANY ROAD
OLD DOVER RD.
REECE ADAMS HOUSE
The Battle Of Britain Memorial
NEW
The Warren
THE WARREN CAMP SITE
EAST CLIFF & WARREN COUNTRY PARK (Nature Reserve)
Martello Tower 1
Zone

A
B
C
D
26
27
22
33
40
39
38
37
1
2
3
4
5
6
Farm
Pond
FORGE FIELD
QUEEN'S LEA
MILL
Street End Farm
Woods
White Hill
CROOK'S CT. LA.
GRAVEL LANE
Bridledown
CHANNEL
Church Hougham
Chalk Pit Wood
T.V. Transmitting Station
Hougham Court
Great Hougham Court Farm
Little Hougham Court
HOUGHAM COURT LANE
B2011
DO
D
SATMAR
Gt. Satmar Farm
Satmar
Dawkinge Wood
A20
Folkestone
CT18
CT15
Court Wood
Abbot's Land Fm.
WHITE CLIFFS PARK
NEW DOVER ROAD
Abbotscliff House
Abbotscliff Tunnel
OLD DOVER RD.
Groynes
ENGLISH

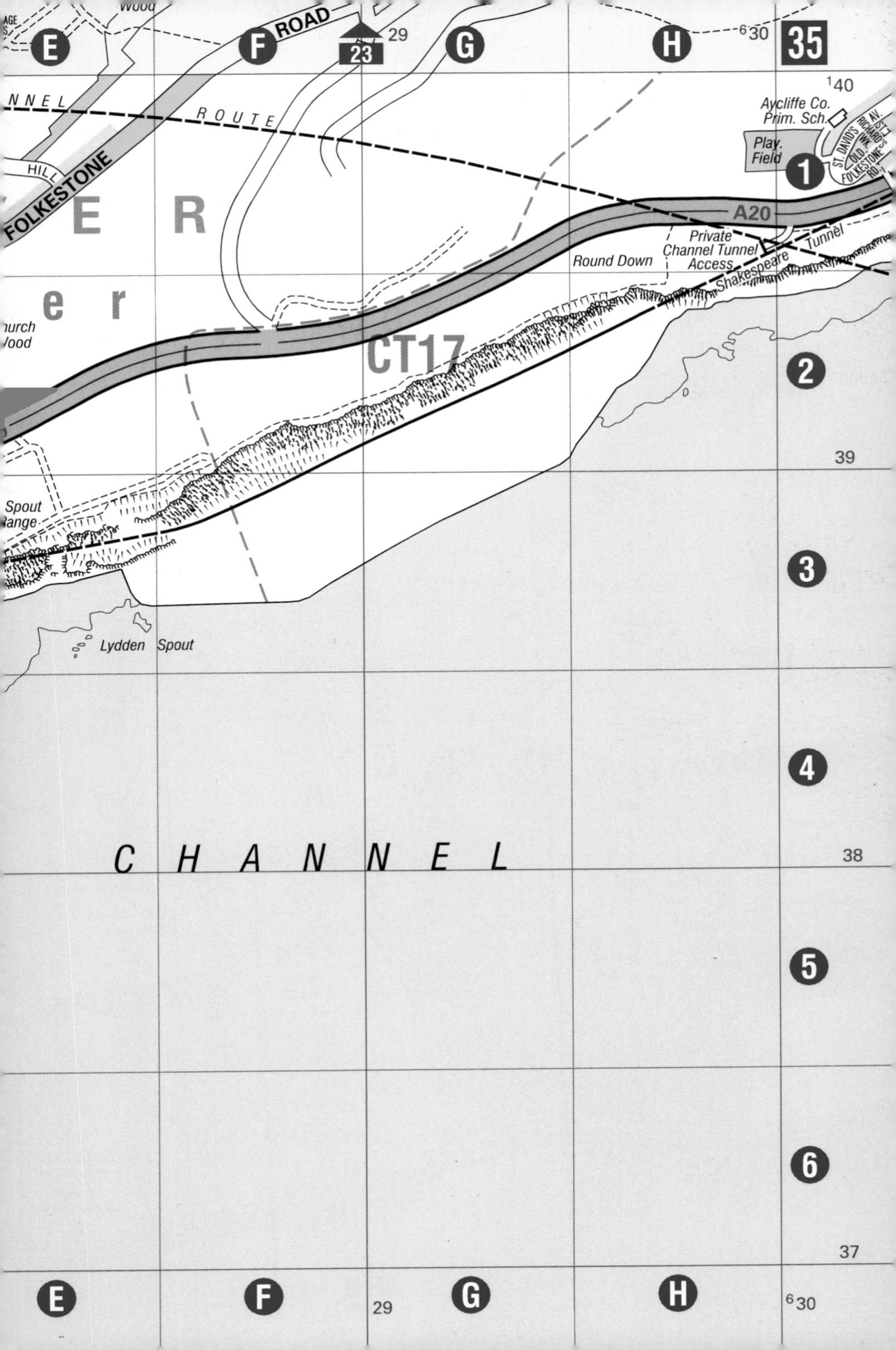

Wood

1 40

N N E L

R O U T E

Aycliffe Co.
Prim. Sch.

St David's Av.

FOLKESTONE RD.

Old Folkestone Rd.

HILL

Play.
Field

1

FOLKESTONE

A20

E R

Private
Channel Tunnel
Access

Shakespeare Tunnel

Round Down

2

e r

urch
ood

CT17

39

3

Spout
ange

4

Lydden Spout

CHANNEL

38

5

6

37

610
A
B
C
D
26
11
37
36
35
34
1
2
3
4
5
6
Humblebee Hall
BARROW HILL
A20
ASHFORD
LANE
B2067
Mink Farm
Otterpool Quarry
Red House Farm
Otterpool Manor
Ashford
TN25
Harringe Brooks Wood
Upper Otterpool
S H E
OTTERPOOL
Coldharbour Cottage
Danehurst Wood
Coldharbour House
Works
LYMPNE INDUSTRIAL ESTATE
AIRFIELD (Private)
Danehurst
Danehill
Danehill Bungalow
ALDINGTON
B2067
ROAD
Lodges
Lodge
Queens Court
Port Lympne House
REACH RD.
ALDINGTON
LYMPNE PLACE COTTS.
Mill House
Lympne Place School
Port Lympne Wild Animal Park
Hill Hurst Wood
REACH ROAD
French House
Combe Farm
Saxon Shore Way
ROYAL
ROYAL
MILITARY
MILITARY
Aldergate Bridge
ALDERGATE LANE
Stutfall Castle (remains of)
Lemanis Roman Fort
CANAL
44
Nook

37
27
45
38
FOLKESTONE RACE COURSE
Westenhanger
Hillhurst Farm
Honeywood Plantation
Honeywood Cottages
Sandling Park
MEADOW CT.
Twin Chimneys
Little Greys
Killymoon
Depot
The Willows
Elms Farm
Newingreen
ASHFORD ROAD
A20
HYTHE ROAD
A261
KILN WOOD
FOLKS' WOOD
Black Hill
Newingreen Farm
Ashford Lodge
Ivy Cottage
Pedlinge
Pedlinge Farm
Oxenden Farm
Berwick House
Berwick Manor Farm
LYMPNE
CT21
Shepmead
Oathill Cottages
Shipway Cross
Shepway Cross
Shepway
Court Wood
BERWICK
OCTAVIAN DR.
ISIS CL.
RIDGEWAY
LANE
ALDINGTON ROAD
OLD
LYMPNE HILL
Lympne Park Wood
West Hythe
West Hythe Water Works
THE ROUGHS
ST. MARY'S
ROYAL MILITARY ROAD
West Hythe Bridge
RIVERSIDE IND. EST.
WOODLAND RISE
WEST HYTHE ROAD
BURMARSH
THE HAVEN
GREBE CRES.
MARTIN'S WY.
DOVE CL.
CHANNEL CARAVAN PK.
OAKLANDS COTTS.
WILLOW TREE FM. CARAVAN PARK
PRINCE OF WALES RES. MOBILE HOME PK.
ELM CT.
Rose Cottage
E
F
G
H
1
2
3
4
5
6
13
14
34
35
36
37

38
ASHFORD RD.
M20 MOTORWAY
28
Sandling
Hayne Barn Equestrian Centre
Heane Wood
House Wood
Sandling Park
Sandling Farm
Rectory Wood
Garden House
American Garden
Foxhole
Willow Wood
Westerlea
Minstead
Deer Paddock
Black Hill
Chesterfield Wood
Saltwood House
Brockhill Park School
Sports Ground
Tennis Courts
Brockhill Park Sch.
BROCKHILL COUNTRY PARK
Brockhill Stream
HYTHE
Pedlinge
Pedlinge Farm
Oxenden Farm
Harp Wood
Woodacres
Redbrooks Wood
The Streams
LONDON ROAD
A261
Court Wood
Orchard Valley
ALDINGTON ROAD
OLD LONDON ROAD
MILITARY ROAD
Hythe
DYMCHURCH ROAD
The Green
Hythe Inf. Sch.
THE ROUGHS
KENGATE IND. EST.
PENNYPOT IND. EST.
A259
Football Ground
Shorncliffe Rifle Ranges
ROYAL MILITARY CANAL ROAD
Pennypot
RANGE ROAD INDUSTRIAL ESTATE
Gas Works
CHANNEL CARAVAN PK.
OAKLANDS COTTS.
PRINCE OF WALES RES. MOBILE HOME PK.
WILLOW TREE FM. CARAVAN PARK
BURMARSH ROAD
Stonecroft
Honeywood Plantation
Honeywood Cottages
Lodge

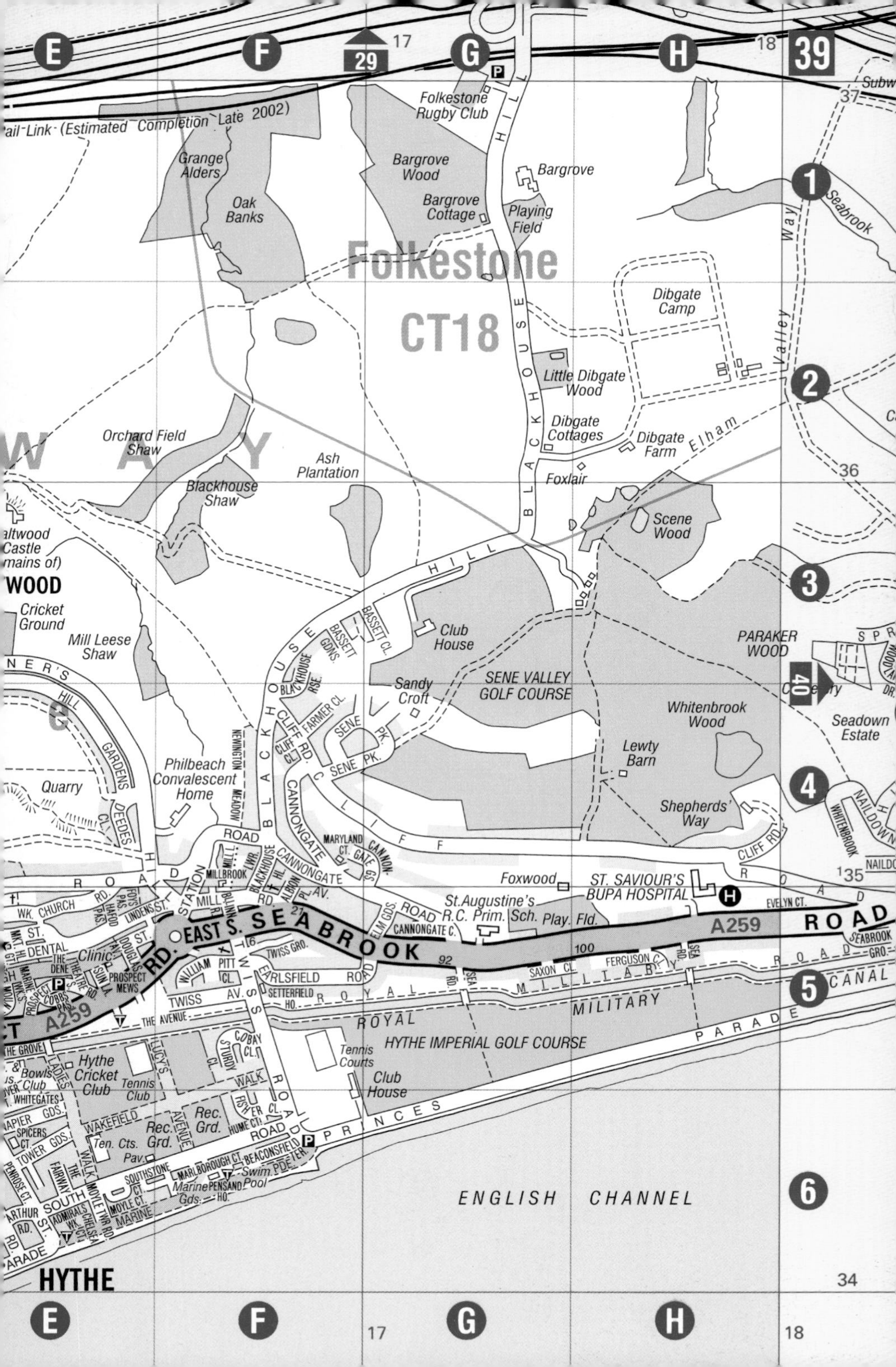

Grid references (top): E F 17 G H 18 39

Grid references (right): 1 2 3 4 5 6

Grid references (bottom): E F 17 G H 18

Folkestone Rugby Club

Bargrove Wood

Bargrove

Grange Alders

Oak Banks

Bargrove Cottage

Playing Field

Dibgate Camp

Folkestone CT18

Little Dibgate Wood

Dibgate Cottages

Dibgate Farm

Foxlair

Elham

Orchard Field Shaw

Ash Plantation

Blackhouse Shaw

Scene Wood

Saltwood Castle (remains of)

WOOD

Cricket Ground

Mill Leese Shaw

Club House

SENE VALLEY GOLF COURSE

PARAKER WOOD

Whitenbrook Wood

Seadown Estate

Sandy Croft

Lewty Barn

Quarry

Philbeach Convalescent Home

Shepherds' Way

CLIFF RD.

Foxwood

ST. SAVIOUR'S BUPA HOSPITAL

EVELYN CT.

St.Augustine's R.C. Prim. Sch. Play. Fld.

EAST S. SEABROOK

A259 ROAD

SEABROOK

CANAL

ROYAL MILITARY

HYTHE IMPERIAL GOLF COURSE

Hythe Cricket Club

Tennis Club

Tennis Courts

Club House

Rec. Grd.

PRINCES

ENGLISH CHANNEL

HYTHE

34

Rail Link (Estimated Completion Late 2002)

40
30
Subway
Superstore
HIGH STREET
Eurotunnel Customer Service Centre
CHERITON ROAD
ROMAN WAY
SAMIAN CR.
TIBER CL.
TOLSFORD CL.
A20 CHERITON
Cheriton C. P. Sch.
CHURCH ROAD
Seabrook
St.Martin's Plain
CT18
CT21
UNDERHILL
BUFFS AV.
FUSILIER AV.
QUEENS AVENUE
BROADVIEW
CHERITON COURT RD.
St. Martin C. of E. Prim. Sch.
Underhill House
VALEBROOK CL.
POND HILL ROAD
The Stadium
Sports Ground
Risborough Barracks
Cricket Grd.
Valley Way
Stream
Casebourne Wood
Casebourne Farm
CRAYTHORNE CL.
VALESTONE CL.
Elham
Hythe
Rec. Grd.
Horn Street
HORN STREET
SEABROOK VALE
NORTH ROAD
B2063
WEST ROAD
Napier Barracks
Shorncliffe Camp
Burgoyne Barracks
Sir John Moore Plain
PARAKER WOOD
PARAKER LANE
SPRING
Cemetery
Whitenbrook Wood
Seadown Estate
HIGH RIDGE
QUARRY WLK.
Play Fld.
HAMPTON VLE.
PARAKER WAY
SPRINGFIELD WY.
Seabrook Stream
WEST RD.
SOUTH RD.
MARTELLO
Martello Tower
UPPER CORNICHE
THE CORNICHE
HILL
Shepherds' Way
CLIFF RD.
NAILDOWN
WHITENBROOK
NAILDOWN CL.
BRIDLE WAY
COLIN'S WY.
VALLEY WK.
BROOK CL.
Seabrook House
SANDY LANE
SEABROOK CT.
HOSPITAL
HELENA CORNICHE
LOWER CORNICHE
LATCHGATE
SPENCER CT.
PEMBERTON CT.
BATTERY PT.
SEABROOK ROAD
A259
THE ROAD
EVELYN CT.
SEABROOK GS.
SEABROOK GRO.
VICTORIA GR.
BEACON TER.
Seapoint Activity Cen.
Courts
A259 ESPLA
ROYAL MILITARY
CANAL
PARADE
PRINCES
Seabrook
ENGLISH

E
F
G
H
31
41
42
36
35
22
21
1
2
3
4
5
6
Morehall Recreation Ground
School
AVENUE
YORK MEWS
SOMERSET RD.
POSTLING RD.
DARLINGHST RD.
STODDART RD.
WELLS RD.
BOWEN RD.
PHILLIP
HARCOURT
CHERRY GARDEN LA.
CHERRY GARDEN AV.
A20
Morehall Co. Prim. Sch.
Playing Field
Broadmead Village
Miniature Golf Course
Folkestone Sports Cen.
Tennis Cts.
Folkestone Cricket Club Ground
The Harvey Gram. Sch. for Girls
Folkestone F.C.
Indoor Bowls Centre
Superstore
CT19
CORNWALLIS AVENUE
RADNOR PARK AV.
ROYAL VICTORIA HOSP.
Bowls Club
Radnor Park
ST. CHERITON ROAD
A2034
NARRABEEN RD.
CHART ROAD
MOREHALL AV.
BROOMFIELD RD.
DUNNETT RD.
GERALDINE RD.
SHORNCLIFFE ROAD
SHORNCLIFFE CRESCENT
Folkestone West
Cemetery
Folkestone Central
Sth. Kent Coll.
St. Mary's Coll.
Westbrook House Sch.
Play. Fld.
B2064
SHORNCLIFFE RD.
EARLS AV.
A259
Adult Ed. Cen.
Civic Centre
Palting Ho.
Law Courts
CASTLE HILL AV.
WEST TERRACE
FREMANTLE
REDMILL CL.
VALLEY ROAD
ENBROOK ROAD
ROMNEY AVENUE
COOLINGE LANE
Coolinge Playing Field
Eversley Coll.
Sandgate C. P. Sch.
Folkestone Sch. For Girls
CT20
HARDWICK RD.
BOUVERIE ROAD
PELHAM GDNS.
GRIMSTON GS.
PLAIN RD.
Playing Field
Martello Tower 5
Martello Tower 6
Martello Tower 4
Rec. Grd.
Offices
SANDGATE HILL
SANDGATE ROAD
SANDGATE HIGH ST.
The Metropole
Balfour Gdns.
RADNOR CLIFF
THE RIVIERA
LOWER SANDGATE ROAD
Castle
Sandgate
CHANNEL

A
B
C
D
1
2
3
4
5
6
32
41
22
23
37
36
35
34
Park Farm C.P. Sch.
Mundella C.P. Sch.
Stella Maris R. C. Prim. Sch.
ROYAL VICTORIA HOSP.
Folkestone Sports Cen.
Miniature Golf Course
Tennis Cts.
Bowls Club
Radnor Park
RADNOR PK. RD.
PAVILION R.
BLACK BULL RD.
FOORD RD.
CANTERBURY RD.
SIDNEY STREET
ALEXANDRA ST.
STUART RD.
Works
Goods Yard
HIGHFIELD IND. EST.
MARTELLO IND. EST.
WARREN
FORELAND
FOLLY RD.
EASTFIELDS
DOVER ROAD
THE TRAM ROAD
RADNOR BRI. RD.
BAY
PARADE
CORONATION
East Pier
Outer Harbour
Folkestone Harbour
Folkestone Harbour Pier
FOLKESTONE
Pier Hd. Lighthouse
CHERITON RD.
Folkestone Central
BROADMEAD
BROCKMAN
CHERITON ROAD
SHORNCLIFFE RD.
CHERITON GDNS.
Civic Centre
Palting Ho.
Law Courts
BOUVERIE R.W.
BOUVERIE ROAD WEST
Bus Sta.
A259
A2033
SANDGATE RD.
Sth. Kent Coll.
TONTINE ST.
DOVER
HIGH ST.
THE BAYLE
THE LANTERNS SHOP. CEN.
ROAD OF REMEMBRANCE
LOWER SANDGATE
MARINE PARADE
Marine Pavilion
PROMENADE
MARINE
Amusement Park
The Leas
Cliff Lift
THE LEAS
THE ROAD
ZIG ZAG PATH
THE SANDGATE
MARINE
Mill Point
EARLS AV.
E N G L I S H

1

2

36

3

4

¹35

C H A N N E L

5

6

34

Martello Tower 3
Visitors' Cen.
(Summer Only)

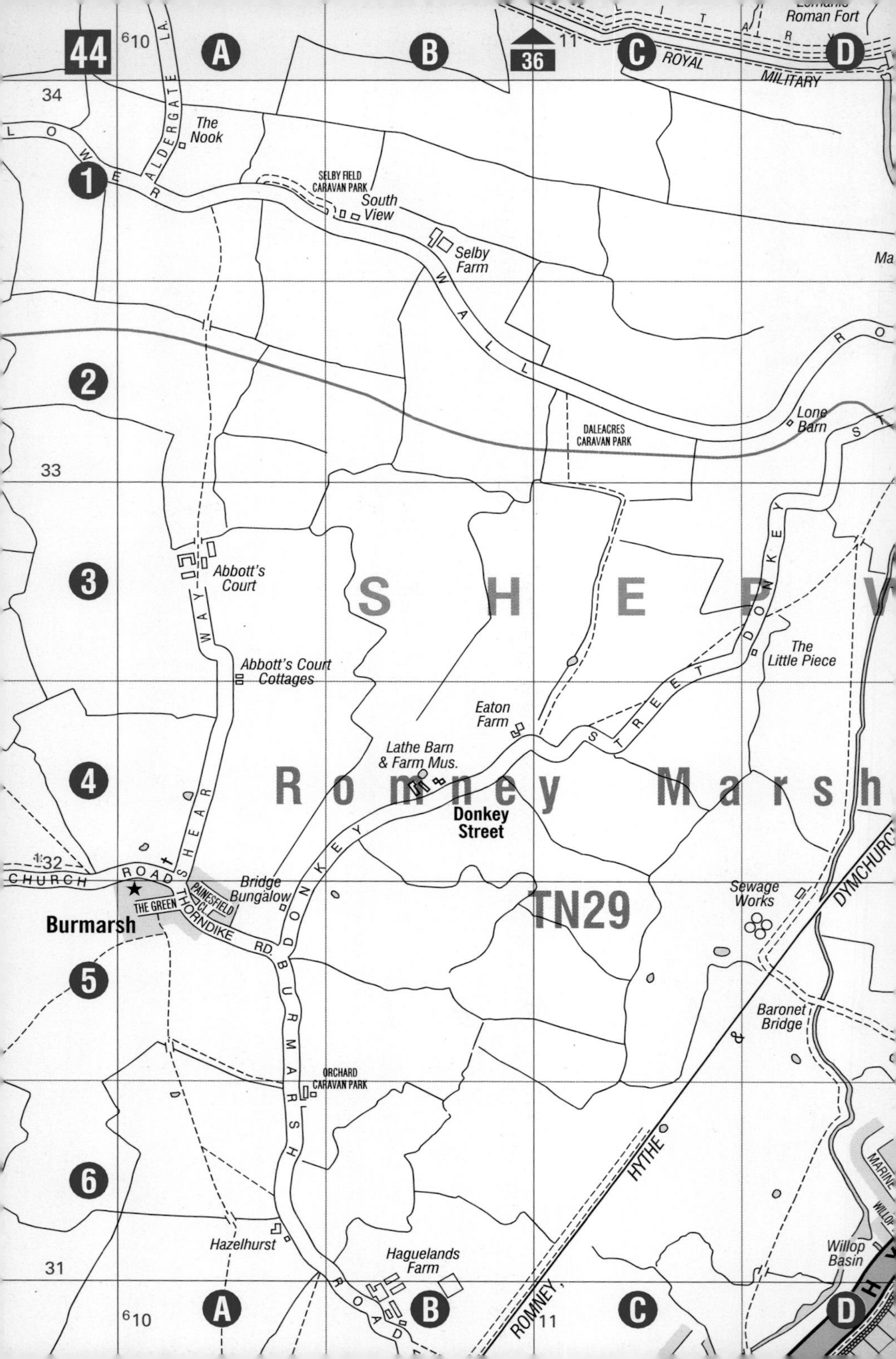

A   B   ▲ 11   C   ROYAL   D
36

Lympne
Roman Fort

L I T T L

34

The
Nook

1

LOWER ALDERGATE LA.

SELBY FIELD
CARAVAN PARK

South
View

Selby
Farm

WALL

ROAD

Ma

2

DALEACRES
CARAVAN PARK

Lone
Barn

ST

33

S   H   E   P   W

3

WAY

Abbott's
Court

DONKEY STREET

The
Little Piece

Abbott's Court
Cottages

Eaton
Farm

R   o   m   n   e   y   M   a   r   s   h

4

SHEAR

Lathe Barn
& Farm Mus.

Donkey
Street

DYMCHURCH

Sewage
Works

↟32

CHURCH   ROAD

Burmarsh

★ THE GREEN

PAINESFIELD

THORNDIKE RD.

Bridge
Bungalow

DONKEY

TN29

5

BURMARSH

Baronet
Bridge

&

ORCHARD
CARAVAN PARK

6

HYTHE

Willop
Basin

MARINE

WILLOP

31

Hazelhurst

Haguelands
Farm

ROMNEY,   11

ROAD

A   610   B   C   D

45
37
E
F
G
H
1
2
3
4
5
6
13
14
33
32
31
34
Bridge
WOODLAND RISE
ROAD
RIVERSIDE IND. EST.
ROAD
MILITARY
Lakeside Farm
HYTHE
Rose Cottage
Willop Sewer (Gill's Pipes Arm)
Cinderella Farm
The Pebbles
Solway Nursery
Hopelands Farm
ROAD
BURMARSH
THE HAVEN
GREBE CRES.
DOVE CL.
AVENUE
MARTIN'S WY.
NIGHTINGALE AV.
ROBIN'S CL.
KINGFISHER
FINCH GRO.
HERON'S WY.
KINGFISHER GDNS.
Rec. Grd.
CHANNEL CARAVAN PK.
OAKLANDS COTTS.
WILLOW TREE FM. CARAVAN PARK
PRINCE OF WALES RES. MOBILE HOME PK.
BLUEWATER CARAVAN PK.
WYCH ELM CT.
ELM WY.
HAWTHORN CL.
SHEPHDS. W.
ST. GEORGES PL.
PALMARSH CR.
Palmarsh C. P. Sch.
JUBILEE CL.
Willop Sewer (Oaks Arm)
Redoubt Sailing Club
PALMBEACH AVENUE
MARSH VIEW
STUDFALL CL.
KEDDOW'S CL.
OAKS VIEW
PALMARSH AVENUE
PALMARSH CR.
PALMARSH
BURMARSH
Botolph's Bridge
Hythe
Sewage Works
BEACH BANK CARAVAN SITE
A259
Danger Area
Stonereach Bridge
CT21
Martello Tower
BRIDGE
ROAD
BAY
RAILWAY
DYMCHURCH ROAD
Depot
Fort Lodge
River Ho.
Dymchurch Redoubt
WOODLAND WY.
BROCKMAN CRES.
REDOUBT WY.
DENHAM CL.
STANLEY CL.
LIVINGSTONE CL.
BEACH R.
WOOD LAND WY.
REDOUBT WAY
UDEN RD.
CRIMOND AV.
BEVERLEY GDNS.
Outfall
Wall
NEW BEACH HOLIDAY CENTRE
ENGLISH CHANNEL

INDEX TO STREETS

Including Industrial Estates and a selection of Subsidiary Addresses.

HOW TO USE THIS INDEX

1. Each street name is followed by its Postal District and then by its map reference; e.g. Abbey Rd. *Alk* —2D **22** is in the Alkham Postal Locality and is to be found in square 2D on page **22**.
A strict alphabetical order is followed in which Av., Rd., St., etc. (though abbreviated) are read in full and as part of the street name; e.g. Aldergate La. appears after Alder Cotts. but before Alder Rd.

2. Streets and a selection of Subsidiary names not shown on the Maps, appear in the index in *Italics* with the thoroughfare to which it is connected shown in brackets; e.g. *Albany Ho. Dover —4D 24 (off Albany Pl.)*

GENERAL ABBREVIATIONS

All : Alley	Clo : Close	Junct : Junction	Rd : Road
App : Approach	Comn : Common	La : Lane	Shop : Shopping
Arc : Arcade	Cotts : Cottages	Lit : Little	S : South
Av : Avenue	Ct : Court	Lwr : Lower	Sq : Square
Bk : Back	Cres : Crescent	Mnr : Manor	Sta : Station
Boulevd : Boulevard	Dri : Drive	Mans : Mansions	St : Street
Bri : Bridge	E : East	Mkt : Market	Ter : Terrace
B'way : Broadway	Embkmt : Embankment	M : Mews	Trad : Trading
Bldgs : Buildings	Est : Estate	Mt : Mount	Up : Upper
Bus : Business	Gdns : Gardens	N : North	Vs : Villas
Cvn : Caravan	Ga : Gate	Pal : Palace	Wlk : Walk
Cen : Centre	Gt : Great	Pde : Parade	W : West
Chu : Church	Grn : Green	Pk : Park	Yd : Yard
Chyd : Churchyard	Gro : Grove	Pas : Passage	
Circ : Circle	Ho : House	Pl : Place	
Cir : Circus	Ind : Industrial	Quad : Quadrant	

POSTTOWN AND POSTAL LOCALITY ABBREVIATIONS

Acr : Acrise	*Etch* : Etchinghill	*Mart* : Martin	*St Mb* : St Margarets Bay
Alk : Alkham	*Ewe M* : Ewell Minnis	*Mart M* : Martin Mill	*Salt* : Saltwood
B Hts : Burgoyne Heights	*Folk* : Folkestone	*M Hor* : Monks Horton	*S'gte* : Sandgate
Burm : Burmarsh	*Gt Mon* : Great Mongeham	*N'grn* : Newingreen	*S'lng* : Sandling
Cap F : Capel-le-Ferne	*Gus* : Guston	*N'tn* : Newington	*S'ndge* : Sellindge
Chu H : Church Hougham	*Hackl* : Hacklinge	*Non* : Nonington	*Shol* : Sholden
Col : Coldred	*H'nge* : Hawkinge	*O'nge* : Ottinge	*Stanf* : Stanford
Deal : Deal	*Hou* : Hougham	*Peene* : Peene	*S'fld* : Swingfield
Dens : Densole	*Hythe* : Hythe	*Post* : Postling	*Temp E* : Temple Ewell
Dover : Dover	*Kear* : Kearsney	*R Min* : Rhodes Minnis	*Walm* : Walmer
Drel : Drellingore	*Kgdn* : Kingsdown	*R'wld* : Ringwould	*Wnhgr* : Westenhanger
Dym : Dymchurch	*Lyd* : Lydden	*Ripp* : Ripple	*W Hou* : West Hougham
E Lan : East Langdon	*Lym* : Lyminge	*River* : River	*W Hyt* : West Hythe
Elham : Elham	*Lymp* : Lympne	*St Mc* : St Margarets-at-Cliffe	*Whitf* : Whitfield

INDEX TO STREETS

Abbey Clo. *Deal* —6E **5**
Abbey Rd. *Alk* —2D **22**
Abbey Rd. *Temp E* —5F **11**
Abbots, The. *Dover* —3C **24**
Abbott Rd. *Folk* —1C **42**
Acre, The. *Whitf* —1H **11**
Addelam Clo. *Deal* —1E **7**
Addelam Rd. *Deal* —1E **7**
Admirals Wlk. *Hythe* —6E **39**
Adrian St. *Dover* —4D **24**
Aerodrome Rd. *H'nge* —1D **30**
Ainsdale Clo. *Folk* —6H **31**
Alamein Clo. *B Hts* —1F **25**
Albany Ho. Dover —4D 24
(off Albany Pl.)
Albany Pl. *Dover* —4D **24**
Albany Rd. *Cap F* —4F **33**
Albatross Lodge. Dover
           —1B **24**
Alberta Clo. *Dover* —6B **12**
Albert Costain Ct. Folk —2B 42
(off Foord Rd.)
Albert La. *Hythe* —6D **38**

Albert Rd. *Deal* —5G **5**
Albert Rd. *Dover* —2D **24**
Albert Rd. *Folk* —1B **42**
Albert Rd. *Hythe* —6D **38**
Albion M. Rd. *Folk* —3B **42**
Albion Rd. *Deal* —3H **5**
Albion Rd. *Folk* —1B **42**
Albion Rd. *Hythe* —5F **39**
Albion Vs. *Folk* —3B **42**
Alder Cotts. *Lymp* —4E **37**
Aldergate La. *W Hyt* —1A **44**
Alder Rd. *Folk* —1A **42**
Aldington Rd. *Lymp* —4A **36**
Alexandra Ct. *Hythe* —6C **38**
Alexandra Gdns. *Folk* —3B **42**
Alexandra Pl. *Dover* —2C **24**
Alexandra Rd. *Cap F* —3F **33**
Alexandra Rd. *Kgdn* —2G **9**
Alexandra Rd. *Walm* —3H **7**
Alexandra St. *Folk* —6C **32**
Alfred Rd. *Dover* —1B **24**
Alfred Row. *Deal* —4H **5**
Alfred Sq. *Deal* —4H **5**

Alison Clo. *Whitf* —3A **12**
Alison Cres. *Whitf* —3A **12**
Alkham Rd. *Alk* —6D **10**
Alkham Valley Rd. *Alk* —6D **10**
Alkham Valley Rd. *Folk*
  (in two parts)   —3A **32**
Allenby Av. *Deal* —6F **5**
Allendale St. *Folk* —1B **42**
Allen Rd. *S'gte* —4D **40**
Alma Rd. *Folk* —2D **40**
Anchor La. *Deal* —5G **5**
Anselm Rd. *Dover* —3A **24**
Anstee Rd. *Dover* —2C **24**
Anzio Cres. *B Hts* —1E **25**
Appledore Cres. *Folk* —6D **30**
Approach Rd. *Dover* —5A **24**
Archcliffe Rd. *Dover* —6C **24**
Archer Rd. *Folk* —1B **42**
Archer's Ct. Rd. *Whitf* —3A **12**
Archery Sq. *Walm* —2H **7**
Ark La. *Deal* —4G **5**
Armourer's Wlk. *Dover* —6A **12**
Arthur Rd. *Deal* —2E **7**

Arthur Rd. *Hythe* —6E **39**
Arthur St. *Folk* —1C **42**
Ash Clo. *Dover* —1H **23**
Ashen Tree La. *Dover* —3E
Ashford Rd. *N'grn* —1C **36**
Ashford Rd. *N'tn* —6A **30**
Ashford Rd. *S'ndge* —4A **28**
Ashley Av. *Folk* —1E **41**
Ashley Ho. *Folk* —1E **41**
Ashley Mill Cotts. Folk —6F
(off Ashley Av.)
Ash Pl. *Folk* —5C **32**
Ashton Clo. *Gt Mon* —1B **6**
Ash Tree Rd. *Folk* —1C **42**
Aspen Ho. *Folk* —3B **42**
Astley Av. *Dover* —4B **24**
Astley Av. *Dover* —6A **30**
Astley Ct. *Dover* —1C **24**
Astor Av. *Dover* —4B **24**
Astor Dri. *Deal* —6G **5**
Astrid Rd. *Walm* —3E **7**
Athelstan Pl. *Deal* —3G **5**
Athelstan Rd. *Folk* —6B **32**
Athol Ter. *Dover* —3F **25**

Canada Rd.—Cornwall Ho.

Canada Rd. *Walm* —1G **7**
Cannongate Av. *Hythe* —4F **39**
Cannongate Clo. *Hythe*
—5G **39**
Cannongate Gdns. *Hythe*
—4G **39**
Cannongate Rd. *Hythe* —4F **39**
Cannon St. *Deal* —4G **5**
Cannon St. *Dover* —3D **24**
Canons Ga. Rd. *Dover* —3E **25**
Canterbury Rd. *Dens & H'nge*
—3G **19**
Canterbury Rd. *Elham* —1F **17**
Canterbury Rd. *Etch* —1F **29**
Canterbury Rd. *Folk* —4A **32**
Canterbury Rd. *Lyd* —2A **10**
Canterbury Rd. *Lym* —4E **17**
Canute Rd. *Deal* —2G **5**
Canute Wlk. *Deal* —2G **5**
Capel Ct. Pk. *Cap F* —3H **33**
Capel St. *Cap F* —3F **33**
(in two parts)
Capstan Row. *Deal* —4H **5**
Carlsden Clo. *Dover* —6A **12**
Carlton Leas. *Folk* —3A **42**
Carlton Rd. *Kgdn* —1G **9**
Carters Rd. *Folk* —2F **41**
Casino Sq. *Gus* —1E **25**
Castalia Cotts. Walm —2H 7
(off Cambridge Rd.)
Castle Av. *Dover* —2D **24**
Castle Av. *Hythe* —4D **38**
Castle Bay. *S'gte* —4C **40**
Castle Clo. *Lymp* —5D **36**
Castle Clo. *S'gte* —4F **41**
Castle Cres. *Salt* —3E **39**
Castle Dri. *Whitf* —3H **11**
Castle Hill. *Folk* —5G **31**
Castle Hill Av. *Folk* —2A **42**
Castle Hill Pas. *Folk* —2A **42**
Castle Hill Rd. *Dover* —2E **25**
Castle M. *Deal* —2F **7**
Castlemount Ct. *Dover* —3E **25**
Castlemount Rd. *Dover*
—2D **24**
Castle Rd. *Salt* —3D **38**
Castle Rd. *S'gte* —4F **41**
Castle St. *Dover* —4D **24**
Castleview Ct. *Dover* —2B **24**
Castle Wlk. *Deal* —2H **5**
Cauldham Clo. *Cap F* —4F **33**
Cauldham La. *Cap F* —3E **33**
Cavell Sq. *Deal* —2E **7**
Cavenagh Rd. *St Mc* —3F **15**
Cecil Rd. *Walm* —6H **7**
Cedar Ct. *Folk* —2E **41**
Cedar Ter. Dover —6B 12
(off Selkirk Rd.)
Celtic Rd. *Deal* —2E **7**
Cemetery Cotts. *H'nge* —1F **31**
Centre Rd. *Dover* —5C **24**
Century Wlk. *Deal* —5G **5**
Chaffinch Lodge. *Dover*
—1B **24**
Chalcroft Rd. *S'gte* —3E **41**
Chalk Clo. *Folk* —6G **31**
Chalk Hill Rd. *Kgdn* —2G **9**
Chalksole Grn. La. *Alk* —1E **21**
Chalkwell Ct. *Dover* —4A **24**
Chamberlain Rd. *Dover*
—3A **24**

Chance Meadow. *Gus* —3F **13**
Channel Cvn. Pk. *Hythe*
—1H **45**
Channel Clo. *Folk* —6D **32**
Channel Lea. *Walm* —4G **7**
Channel View. Folk —2C 42
(off North St.)
Channel View Rd. *Dover*
—5C **24**
Chapel La. Dover —4D 24
(off York St.)
Chapel La. *R Min* —1C **16**
Chapel La. *Ripp* —5B **6**
Chapel La. *St Mc* —3D **14**
Chapel Pl. *Dover* —4D **24**
Chapel Rd. *Whitf* —1A **12**
Chapel St. *Deal* —5H **5**
Chapel St. *Hythe* —5D **38**
Chapel Wlk. Dover —3D 24
(off Priory Rd.)
Chapman Ho. *Deal* —2F **7**
Charles Cres. *Folk* —6E **31**
Charles Ho. *Deal* —2F **7**
Charles Lister Ct. *Dover*
—2B **24**
Charles Rd. *Deal* —1F **7**
Charlotte St. *Folk* —2C **42**
Charlton Arc. Dover —3C 24
(off High St. Dover,)
Charlton Av. *Dover* —2C **24**
Charlton Grn. *Dover* —2C **24**
Chart Rd. *Folk* —1F **41**
Chase, The. *St Mc* —1D **14**
Chater Ct. *Deal* —1G **7**
Chaucer Cres. *Dover* —6B **12**
Chelsea Ct. *Hythe* —6E **39**
Cheriton Ct. Rd. *Folk* —1C **40**
Cheriton Gdns. *Folk* —2A **42**
Cheriton High St. *Folk* —1B **40**
Cheriton Pl. *Folk* —3B **42**
Cheriton Pl. *Walm* —1H **7**
Cheriton Rd. *Folk* —1F **41**
Cheriton Rd. *Walm* —1H **7**
Cheriton Wood Ho. *Folk*
—6D **30**
Cherry Brook Rd. *Folk* —1E **41**
Cherry Ct. *Folk* —1G **41**
Cherry Garden Av. *Folk*
—1G **41**
Cherry Garden La. *Folk*
—6F **31**
Cherry Gdns. *Elham* —1H **17**
Cherry La. *Gt Mon* —2B **6**
Cherry Tree Av. *Dover* —2C **24**
Chestnut Clo. *Hythe* —6A **38**
Chestnut Clo. *Whitf* —1A **12**
Chestnut Rd. *Dover* —4B **24**
Chestnut Ter. *Hythe* —6C **38**
Chevalier Rd. *Dover* —4A **24**
Chichester Pl. Elham —2H 17
(off New Rd.)
Chichester Rd. *S'gte* —3E **41**
Chilham Rd. *Folk* —1E **41**
Chilton Av. *Temp E* —6E **11**
Chilton Ct. *Folk* —1C **42**
Chilton Way. *Dover* —6F **11**
Chislett Clo. *S'ndge* —3C **26**
Chisnall Rd. *Dover* —5G **11**
Christchurch Ct. *Dover*
—4D **24**
Christ Chu. Rd. *Folk* —2A **42**

Christchurch Way. *Dover*
—6B **12**
Church Cliff. *Kgdn* —1H **9**
Church Ct. *Lym* —5E **17**
Church Field. *Stanf* —4F **27**
Church Haven. *R'wld* —2D **8**
Church Hill. *Hythe* —5E **39**
Church Hill. *Temp E* —4F **11**
Church Ho. *Deal* —4G **5**
Churchill Av. *Folk* —5G **31**
Churchill Av. *Walm* —3G **7**
Churchill Clo. *Folk* —5B **32**
Churchill Clo. *St Mc* —4D **14**
Churchill Ct. *Hythe* —6D **38**
Churchill Ho. Dover —6B 12
(off Hudson Clo.)
Churchill Ho. Folk —2F 41
(off Coolinge La.)
Churchill Rd. *Dover* —5A **24**
Churchill St. *Dover* —2C **24**
Churchill Wlk. *H'nge* —1F **31**
Church La. *Chu H* —6D **22**
Church La. *Lyd* —2A **10**
Church La. *M Hor* —1D **26**
Church La. *R'wld* —2D **8**
Church La. *Ripp* —5B **6**
Church La. *Shol & Deal* —6D **4**
(in two parts)
Church Meadows. *Deal* —5E **5**
Church Path. *Deal* —1E **7**
(in three parts)
Church Path. *Gt Mon* —2B **6**
Church Path. *Walm* —4G **7**
Church Pl. *Dover* —3D **24**
Church Rd. *Burm* —5A **44**
Church Rd. *Dover* —4A **24**
Church Rd. *Folk* —1C **40**
Church Rd. *Hythe* —5E **39**
Church Rd. *Lym* —4E **17**
Church St. *Dover* —4D **24**
Church St. *Folk* —3B **42**
Church St. *Walm* —4F **7**
Church Wlk. Elham —2H 17
(off Pound La.)
Church Whitfield Rd. *Wald*
—1B **12**
Cinque Ports Av. *Hythe*
—6D **38**
Circular Rd. *Dover* —2H **25**
Citadel Cres. *Dover* —5B **24**
Citadel Heights. *Dover* —5B **24**
Citadel Rd. *Dover* —5B **24**
Clanwilliam Rd. *Deal* —6H **5**
Claremont Clo. *Kgdn* —1G **9**
Claremont Rd. *Deal* —6F **5**
Claremont Rd. *Folk* —2A **42**
Claremont Rd. *Kgdn* —1G **9**
Clarence Pl. *Deal* —4H **5**
Clarence Pl. *Dover* —6D **24**
Clarence Rd. *Cap F* —4F **33**
Clarence Rd. *Walm* —2H **7**
Clarence St. *Folk* —2B **42**
Clarendon Pl. *Dover* —4C **24**
Clarendon Rd. *Dover* —4C **24**
Clarendon St. *Dover* —4B **24**
Clarkes Clo. *Deal* —1D **6**
Cleveland Clo. *Dover* —6B **12**
Cliff Clo. *Hythe* —4F **39**
Cliffe Ho. *Folk* —4G **41**
Cliffe Path. *St Mc* —6C **14**
Cliffe Rd. *Kgdn* —1H **9**

Clifford Gdns. *Deal* —3F **7**
Clifford Pk. Cvn. Site. *Walm*
—5F
Cliff Rd. *Folk* —4G **41**
Cliff Rd. *Hythe* —4F **39**
Cliffstone Ct. *Folk* —2H **41**
Clifton Cres. *Folk* —4H **41**
Clifton Gdns. *Folk* —3A **42**
Clifton Mans. *Folk* —3A **42**
Clifton Rd. *Folk* —3A **42**
Clim Down. *Kgdn* —1H **9**
Close, The. Folk —5B 32
(off Fleming Way)
Close, The. *Lyd* —1B **10**
Close, The. *Salt* —3D **38**
Coach Rd. *Acr* —3E **19**
Coastguard Cotts. *Dover*
—3G **2**
Coastguard Cotts. *Hythe*
—6D **3**
Coastguard Cotts. *Kgdn* —3H
Cobay Clo. *Hythe* —5F **39**
Cobbs M. Folk —3A 42
(off Christ Chu. Rd.)
Cobbs Pas. *Hythe* —5E **39**
Cobden Rd. *Folk* —1E **41**
Cobden Rd. *Hythe* —6D **38**
Cock La. *Elham* —2H **17**
Coldblow Rd. *Walm* —5E **7**
Coldred Hill. *Col* —1B **10**
Colin's Way. *Hythe* —4A **40**
Collards La. *Elham* —3G **17**
College Rd. *Deal* —3H **5**
College Row. Dover —4B 24
(off Elms Vale Rd.)
Collingwood Ct. Folk —2E 41
(off Collingwood Rise)
Collingwood Rise. *Folk* —2E **4**
Collingwood Rd. *St Mc*
—1C **1**
Collingwood Rd. E. *St Mc*
—6E
Colorado Clo. *Dover* —6B **12**
Colton Cres. *Dover* —5B **12**
Common La. *Dover* —6G **11**
Coniston Rd. *Folk* —1H **41**
Connaught Rd. *Dover* —2D **2**
Connaught Rd. *Folk* —2B **42**
Constables Rd. *Dover* —2E **2**
Constable View. *Walm* —2G
Convent Clo. *St Mc* —3E **15**
Conway Clo. *Salt* —3D **38**
Coolinge La. *Folk* —2F **41**
Coolinge Rd. *Folk* —2A **42**
Coombe Clo. *Dover* —2A **24**
Coombe Ct. *Dover* —2A **24**
Coombe Rd. *Dover* —4D **22**
(in two parts)
Coombe Rd. *Folk* —1F **41**
Coombe Valley Rd. *Dover*
Coombe Way. *H'nge* —1A **3**
Coombe Wood La. *H'nge*
—1A **3**
Coppin St. *Deal* —5H **5**
Copthall Gdns. *Folk* —2B **42**
Cordova Ct. *Folk* —3F **41**
Corniche, The. *S'gte* —4C **4**
Cornwall Ho. *Deal* —6E **5**
Cornwall Ho. Dover —4D 24
(off Military Rd.)

Fenner Clo. *S'gte* —3E **41**
Fenton Ct. *Shol* —5F **5**
Ferguson Clo. *Hythe* —5H **39**
Fern Bank Cres. *Folk* —1B **42**
Fern Clo. *H'nge* —5A **20**
Ferne La. *Ewe M* —6A **10**
Ferne Way. *Folk* —1E **41**
Fernfield. *H'nge* —5A **20**
Fernfield La. *H'nge* —5A **20**
Finch Gro. *Hythe* —1H **45**
Finch M. *Deal* —1G **7**
Findley Ct. *Hythe* —5D **38**
Firs Clo. *Folk* —1D **40**
Firs La. *Folk* —1D **40**
Firs, The. *Deal* —3H **5**
Fisher Clo. *Hythe* —6F **39**
Fishmonger's La. *Dover*
—4E **25**
Fitzwalter Ct. *Dover* —5B **12**
Fiveways Rise. *Deal* —6D **4**
Fleet Rd. *St Mc* —6E **9**
Fleming Way. *Folk* —5B **32**
Florida Clo. *Dover* —6B **12**
Flying Horse La. *Dover* —4E **25**
Folkestone Rd. *Chu H* —1E **35**
Folly Rd. *Folk* —1C **42**
Foord Rd. *Folk* —2B **42**
Foord Rd. N. *Folk* —1B **42**
Foord Rd. S. *Folk* —2B **42**
Foreland Av. *Folk* —1D **42**
Foreland Ct. *St Mc* —4E **15**
Forelands Sq. *Deal* —2F **7**
Forester's Way. *Folk* —2B **42**
Forge Clo. *S'ndge* —4B **26**
Forge Field. *W Hou* —6A **22**
Forge La. *Whitf* —1H **11**
Forge Path. *Whitf* —1A **12**
Fort Rd. *Hythe* —5C **38**
Fosters Clo. *Folk* —6E **31**
Foster Way. *Deal* —6F **5**
Fox Clo. *Lym* —4D **16**
Fox Holt Rd. *S'fld* —1G **19**
Foys Pas. *Hythe* —5E **39**
Frampton Rd. *Hythe* —5C **38**
France Rd. *Whitf* —4A **12**
Frederick Rd. *Deal* —2E **7**
Freedown, The. *St Mc* —2E **15**
Freeman's Way. *Deal* —2F **7**
Fremantle Rd. *Folk* —2E **41**
Freshfield La. *Salt* —3C **38**
Friar's Way. *Dover* —6A **12**
Frith Rd. *Dover* —2C **24**
Front St. *R'wld* —2D **8**
Front, The. *St Mb* —6E **15**
Fulbert Rd. *Dover* —4B **12**
Fusilier Av. *Folk* —1B **40**

Gainsborough Clo. *Folk*
—6G **31**
Gallow's Corner. *Hythe*
—5C **38**
Gaol La. Dover —4D **24**
(off Queen St.)
Garden Rd. *Folk* —1B **42**
Garden Wlk. *Deal* —4G **5**
Gateway, The. *Dover* —4E **25**
Gaunt's Clo. *Deal* —1E **7**
George All. *Deal* —5H **5**
George Gurr Cres. *Folk*
—5B **32**

George La. *Folk* —3B **42**
George St. *Dover* —2B **24**
Geraldine Rd. *Folk* —1F **41**
Gerald Palmby Ct. *Deal* —4G **5**
Gibraltar La. *H'nge* —2E **31**
Gibralter Sq. *Gus* —6E **13**
Gilbert Pl. *S'gte* —4E **41**
Gilford Rd. *Deal* —6G **5**
Gilham Gro. *Deal* —1F **7**
Gillman Clo. *H'nge* —1F **31**
Glack Rd. *Deal* —1D **6**
Glade, The. *Shol* —5D **4**
Gladstone Rd. *Folk* —1C **42**
Gladstone Rd. *Walm* —2G **7**
Glebe Clo. *St Mc* —3D **14**
Glebelands *Alk* —2H **21**
(in two parts)
Glenfield Rd. *Dover* —6B **12**
Glen Gro. *Dover* —4B **24**
Glen Rd. *Kgdn* —1G **9**
Gloster Ropewalk. *Dover*
—6C **24**
Gloster Way. *Dover* —6C **24**
Gloucester Pl. *Folk* —2B **42**
Godwin Rd. *Dover* —3F **25**
Godwyn Ct. *Dover* —2D **24**
Godwyne Clo. *Dover* —3D **24**
Godwyne Path. *Dover* —2D **24**
Godwyne Rd. *Dover* —3D **24**
Godwyn Rd. *Deal* —3G **5**
Godwyn Rd. *Folk* —2G **41**
Golden St. *Deal* —4H **5**
Golf Ct. *Deal* —2G **5**
Golf Rd. *Deal* —1G **5**
Goodfellow Way. *Dover*
—3D **24**
Good Hope. *Deal* —1D **6**
Goodwin Rd. *St Mb* —5D **14**
Gordon Rd. *Folk* —1D **40**
Gordon Rd. *Whitf* —4A **12**
Gorley Ho. *Dover* —4D **24**
Goschen Rd. *Dover* —3B **24**
Gothic Clo. *Walm* —4F **7**
Gough Rd. *S'gte* —4E **41**
Grace Hill. *Folk* —2B **42**
Grace Meadow. *Whitf* —2H **11**
Grace Wlk. *Deal* —6E **5**
Gram's Rd. *Walm* —4F **7**
Grand Ct. Folk —4H **41**
(off Earls Av.)
Grange Ct. Folk —3A **42**
(off Ingles Rd.)
Grange Rd. *Deal* —6F **5**
Grange Rd. *Folk* —1E **41**
Grange Rd. *Salt* —3D **38**
Grantham Av. *Deal* —6E **5**
Granville Pde. *S'gte* —4E **41**
Granville Rd. *Kgdn* —4H **9**
Granville Rd. *St Mb* —4E **15**
Granville Rd. *Walm* —3G **7**
Granville Rd. E. *S'gte* —4F **41**
Granville Rd. W. *S'gte* —4E **41**
Granville St. *Deal* —6H **5**
Granville St. *Dover* —2C **24**
Grasmere Gdns. *Folk* —6H **31**
Gravel La. *W Hou* —1B **34**
Gt. Conduit St. *Folk* —5E **39**
Grebe Clo. *H'nge* —1G **31**
Grebe Cres. *Hythe* —1G **45**
Greenacre Dri. *Walm* —4G **7**
Greenbanks. *Lym* —5E **17**

Green Ct. *Folk* —6C **32**
Greenfield Cotts. *S'ndge*
—3C **26**
Greenfield Rd. *Folk* —6C **32**
Greenfields. *S'ndge* —3C **26**
Greengates. *Whitf* —1A **12**
Green La. *CT15* —1H **21**
Green La. *Dover* —1B **24**
Green La. *Folk* —1C **42**
Green La. *Hythe* —5C **38**
Green La. *R Min* —2A **16**
Green La. *St Mc* —1C **14**
Green La. *Temp E* —4F **11**
(in two parts)
Green La. *Walm* —4F **7**
Green La. Av. *Hythe* —5C **38**
Green, The. *Burm* —5A **44**
Green, The. *Salt* —3D **38**
Greenwich La. *Ewe M* —5A **10**
Griffin St. *Deal* —4H **5**
Grimston Av. *Folk* —2H **41**
Grimston Gdns. *Folk* —3H **41**
Grosvenor Ter. Folk —1C **42**
(off Tram Rd., The)
Grote Ct. Folk —2B **42**
(off Dover Rd.)
Grove Rd. *Folk* —2C **42**
Grove Rd. *Walm* —2H **7**
Grove Ter. Folk —1C **42**
(off Dover Rd.)
Grove, The. *Deal* —5G **5**
Grove, The. *Dover* —2C **24**
Grove, The. *Hythe* —5E **39**
Guildford Ct. *Walm* —3H **7**
Guildhall St. *Folk* —2B **42**
Guildhall St. N. *Folk* —2B **42**
Guilford Av. *Whitf* —1H **11**
Gurling Rd. *St Mc* —6D **8**
Guston Rd. *Dover* —2E **25**
Guthrie Gdns. *Dover* —6G **11**

Hacklinge Rd. *Deal* —1A **4**
Hafod Pas. *Hythe* —5E **39**
Hall Cres. *Shol* —6D **4**
Halliday Ct. *Hythe* —5C **38**
Halstatt Rd. *Deal* —2E **7**
Halt, The. *Elham* —2H **17**
Hamilton Rd. *Deal* —1F **7**
Hamilton Rd. *Dover* —3A **24**
Hamlets, The. *Dover* —3B **24**
Hammonds Rd. *Folk* —2E **41**
Hampton Vale. *Hythe* —3B **40**
Hancocks Field. *Deal* —6E **5**
Hangman's La. *R'wld* —2B **8**
(in two parts)
Hanover Clo. *Walm* —3H **7**
Hanover Ct. Folk —3A **42**
(off Court App.)
Hanover Ct. *Hythe* —6E **39**
Harbour App. Rd. *Folk* —3C **42**
Harbour St. *Folk* —2C **42**
Harbour Way. *Folk* —2C **42**
Harcourt Rd. *Folk* —6F **31**
Hardwicke Rd. *Dover* —5B **24**
Hardwick Rd. *Folk* —3G **41**
Hardy Rd. *St Mc* —1C **14**
Harleighbury Rd. *St Mc*
—3D **14**
Harman Av. *Lymp* —4D **36**
Harold Pas. *Dover* —3E **25**

Harold Rd. *Deal* —3G **5**
Harold's Rd. *Dover* —3E **25**
Harold St. *Dover* —3D **24**
Harpswood La. *Hythe* —4C **3**
Harriot Clo. *Folk* —6H **31**
Hart Clo. *H'nge* —1G **31**
Harvey Pl. Folk —2B **42**
(off Rendezvous St.)
Harvey St. *Folk* —2C **42**
Hasborough Rd. *Folk* —1D **4**
Haskard Clo. *H'nge* —1F **31**
Havelock Rd. *Walm* —2G **7**
Haven Dri. *H'nge* —1G **31**
Haven, The. *Hythe* —6G **37**
Hawkesbury St. *Dover* —6D **2**
Hawkesdown Rd. *Walm* —5G
Hawkins Rd. *Folk* —1D **40**
Hawksdown. *Walm* —5F **7**
Hawkshill Rd. *Walm* —5H **7**
Hawthorn Clo. *Dover* —1G **2**
Hawthorn Clo. *Hythe* —6A **3**
Hayton Rd. *Stanf* —4E **27**
Hayward Clo. *Deal* —1E **7**
Hazeldown Clo. *River* —1G **2**
Heathfield Av. *Dover* —1B **24**
Heights Ter. *Dover* —5C **24**
Helena Corniche. *S'gte* —4C **4**
Helena Rd. *Cap F* —3G **33**
Helena Vs. *S'gte* —4B **40**
Hempton Hill. *M Hor* —1G **2**
Hengist Rd. *Deal* —4H **5**
Henniker Clo. *Whitf* —4H **11**
Herbert St. *Dover* —2B **24**
Herdson Rd. *Folk* —2G **41**
Heritage Rd. *Folk* —1D **40**
Hermitage Clo. *Hythe* —5D **3**
Heron Forstall Av. *H'nge*
—1H **3**
Heron Lodge. *Dover* —1B **24**
Heron's Way. *Hythe* —1G **45**
Herschell Rd. E. *Walm* —2G
Herschell Rd. W. *Walm* —2G
Herschell Sq. *Walm* —2G **7**
Hewitt Rd. *Dover* —3D **24**
Heyford Clo. *H'nge* —1H **31**
Highfield Clo. *Salt* —3C **38**
Highfield Ind. Est. *Folk* —1D **4**
Highland Clo. *Folk* —3F **41**
High Meadow. *Dover* —2C **2**
Highridge. *Hythe* —4A **40**
High St. Deal, *Deal* —4H **5**
High St. Dover, *Dover* —3C **2**
High St. Elham, *Elham* —2H **1**
High St. Hythe, *Hythe* —5D **3**
High St. Lyminge, *Lym*
—5D **1**
High St. St Margaret's at Cliff
St Mc —3D **1**
High St. Temple Ewell, *Temp*
—4F **1**
Hill Clo. *St Mc* —4D **14**
Hillcrest Gdns. *Deal* —3E **7**
Hillcrest Rd. *Hythe* —4D **38**
Hillcrest Rd. *Kgdn* —3G **9**
Hill La. *Peene* —5B **30**
Hill Rd. *Folk* —5B **32**
(in two parts)
Hillside. *S'gte* —4E **41**
Hillside Ct. *Hythe* —5E **39**
Hillside Rd. *Dover* —1A **24**
Hillside St. *Hythe* —5D **38**

Lympne Ind. Est. *Lymp* —4C **36**
Lympne Pl. Cotts. *Hythe* —5C **36**
Lyndhurst Rd. *River* —1G **23**
Lyndon Way. *Lym* —4E **17**
Lynton Rd. *Hythe* —6E **39**
Lynwood. *Folk* —6A **32**
Lysander Way. *H'nge* —1G **31**

McDonald Rd. *Dover* —2A **24**
Mackenzie Dri. *Folk* —2D **40**
Mackenzie Ter. *Dover* —6B **12**
(off Selkirk Rd.)
Mackeson Ct. Hythe —5D **38**
(off Military Rd.)
Madeira Ct. *Folk* —4H **41**
Magdala Rd. *Dover* —2B **24**
Magness Rd. *Deal* —3E **7**
Magpie La. *R Min* —1D **16**
Magpie Lodge. Dover —1B **24**
(off Mayfield Av.)
Maine Clo. *Dover* —6B **12**
Maison Dieu Gdns. *Dover* —3D **24**
Maison Dieu Pl. *Dover* —3D **24**
Maison Dieu Rd. *Dover* —3D **24**
Majestic Pde. *Folk* —3A **42**
Mall, The. *Dover* —3C **24**
Malmains Rd. *Dover* —4A **24**
Malthouse Hill. *Hythe* —5D **38**
Maltings, The. *Walm* —5F **7**
Malvern Cotts. *Kear* —5G **11**
Malvern Meadow. *Temp E* —4G **11**
Malvern Rd. *Dover* —4C **24**
Malvern Rd. *Temp E* —4G **11**
Manger's La. *Dover* —1A **24**
Mangers Pl. *Dover* —6A **12**
Manitoba Ho. Dover —6C **12**
(off Winnipeg Clo.)
Manley Clo. *Whitf* —2A **12**
Manley Ho. *Whitf* —2A **12**
Mannering Clo. *River* —6H **11**
Manor Av. *Deal* —1F **7**
Manor Clo. *Deal* —1E **7**
Manor M. *R'wld* —2D **8**
Manor Rise. *Dover* —5A **24**
Manor Rd. *Deal* —1E **7**
Manor Rd. *Dover* —5A **24**
Manor Rd. *Folk* —3A **42**
Manor Way. *Folk* —3A **42**
Mansion Gdns. *Whitf* —5A **12**
Mantles Hill. *Ripp* —4B **6**
Maple Dri. *H'nge* —6A **20**
Maresfield Clo. *Dover* —1B **24**
Margaret St. *Folk* —2C **42**
Marina Ct. *Deal* —3H **5**
Marina, The. *Deal* —2H **5**
Marine Av. *Dym* —6D **44**
Marine Ct. *Dover* —4E **25**
Marine Cres. *Folk* —3B **42**
Marine Pde. *Dover* —4E **25**
(in two parts)
Marine Pde. *Folk* —3B **42**
Marine Pde. *Hythe* —6E **39**
Marine Pde. M. *Folk* —3C **42**
Marine Point. *Folk* —4G **41**

Marine Promenade. *Folk* —3B **42**
Marine Rd. *Walm* —1H **7**
Marine Ter. *Folk* —3C **42**
Marine Wlk. *Folk* —4H **41**
Marine Wlk. S. *Hythe* —5E **39**
Marjan Clo. *Dover* —2A **24**
Market Hill. *Hythe* —5E **39**
Market Pl. *Folk* —2B **42**
Market Sq. *Dover* —4D **24**
Market St. *Deal* —5H **5**
Market St. *Dover* —4D **24**
Markland Rd. *Dover* —4H **23**
Marlborough Ct. *Folk* —3H **41**
(off Earls Av.)
Marlborough Ct. *Hythe* —6F **39**
Marlborough Rd. *Deal* —3E **7**
Marlborough Rd. *Dover* —4H **23**
Marler Rd. *Folk* —1E **41**
Marlowe Rd. *Dover* —6B **12**
Marshall St. *Folk* —6B **32**
Marsh La. *Shol* —5D **4**
Marsh View. *Hythe* —1G **45**
Martello Cotts. *Hythe* —6A **38**
Martello Dri. *Hythe* —6B **38**
Martello Ind. Est. *Folk* —1D **42**
Martello Rd. *Folk* —1C **42**
(Dover Rd.)
Martello Rd. *Folk* —4D **40**
(West Rd.)
Martello Ter. *S'gte* —4F **41**
Marten Rd. *Folk* —2H **41**
Martha Clo. *Folk* —6H **31**
Martin Dale Cres. Mart H —5A **8**
(off Lucerne La.)
Martin's Way. *Hythe* —1H **45**
Mary Ann Cotts. Folk —6E **31**
(off Ashley Av.)
Maryland Ct. *Hythe* —4F **39**
Mary Rd. *Deal* —2E **7**
Masons Rd. *Dover* —2B **24**
Matthews Clo. *Deal* —5G **5**
Matthew's Pl. *Dover* —2C **24**
Maxton Ct. *Dover* —5A **24**
Maxton Rd. *Dover* —5A **24**
Maxwell Pl. *Deal* —1G **7**
Mayers Rd. *Walm* —4E **7**
Mayfield Av. *Dover* —1B **24**
Mayfield Ct. *Dover* —1B **24**
Mayfield Gdns. *Dover* —1C **24**
Mayfield Rd. *Lym* —5E **17**
Mayfield Rd. *Whitf* —3A **12**
Mayfly Dri. *H'nge* —1G **31**
Meade, The. *H'nge* —1F **31**
Meadowbrook. *S'gte* —3E **41**
Meadowbrook Ct. *S'gte* —3E **41**
Meadow Ct. *Wnhgr* —1F **37**
Meadow Gro. *S'ndge* —5B **26**
Mead Rd. *Folk* —1B **42**
Meadway. *Dover* —6F **11**
Meggett La. *Alk* —3F **21**
Megone Clo. *H'nge* —1G **31**
Melbourne Av. *Dover* —4B **12**
Menzies Av. *Walm* —4F **7**
Meryl Gdns. *Walm* —4G **7**
Metropole Rd. E. *Folk* —4H **41**
Metropole Rd. W. *Folk* —4H **41**
Metropole, The. *Folk* —4H **41**

Middleburg Ho. *Folk* —1D **40**
Middleburg Sq. *Folk* —3B **42**
Middle Deal Rd. *Deal* —6E **5**
Middle Mead. *Folk* —6H **31**
Middle St. *Deal* —5H **5**
Mildred Cotts. *Folk* —6F **31**
Milestone Clo. *Folk* —6G **31**
Military Rd. *Dover* —4D **24**
Military Rd. *Folk* —2D **40**
Military Rd. *Hythe* —5C **38**
Millais Rd. *Dover* —2C **24**
Mill Bay. *Folk* —2B **42**
Millbrook. *Hythe* —4F **39**
Mill Clo. *Dover* —1H **23**
Mill Cotts. *Temp E* —4F **11**
Milldale Clo. *Deal* —1F **7**
Miller Clo. *Deal* —3G **5**
Mill Field. *Folk* —3A **42**
Millfield. *H'nge* —5A **20**
Millfield. *St Mc* —2D **14**
Millfield Clo. *H'nge* —6H **19**
Mill Fields Rd. *Hythe* —5B **38**
Mill Hill. *Deal* —3E **7**
Millhill. *O'nge* —1F **17**
Mill La. *Dover* —4E **25**
Mill La. *H'nge* —1H **31**
Mill La. *Hythe* —4F **39**
Mill La. *Non* —6B **22**
Mill La. *Whitf* —1A **12**
Mill M. *Deal* —1F **7**
Mill Rd. *Deal* —1F **7**
Mill Rd. *Hythe* —5F **39**
Millstone Rd. *Deal* —6F **5**
Mill St. *Temp E* —4F **11**
Milton Clo. *Dover* —5B **12**
Milton Rd. *Dover* —5B **12**
Minerva Av. *Dover* —1C **24**
Minnis La. *Dover* —2D **22**
Minnis Ter. *Dover* —1A **24**
Minter Av. *Dens* —4F **19**
Minter Clo. *Dens* —4F **19**
Mintres Ind. Est. *Deal* —5G **5**
Missenden Ct. Folk —2B **42**
(off Clarence St.)
Mitchell St. *Folk* —1D **40**
Moat Farm Clo. *Folk* —6A **32**
Moat Farm Rd. *Folk* —6A **32**
Mongeham Chu. Clo. *Gt Mon* —2B **6**
Mongeham Rd. *Deal* —4B **6**
Monins Rd. *Dover* —4B **24**
Monks Way. *Dover* —6A **12**
Montague Ct. *Folk* —3H **41**
Montcalm Ter. Dover —6C **12**
(off Winnipeg Clo.)
Montgomery Way. *Folk* —5B **32**
Montreal Clo. *Dover* —6B **12**
Moorstock La. *S'ndge* —4A **26**
Morehall Av. *Folk* —1F **41**
Morrison Rd. *Folk* —1C **42**
Mortimer Rd. *Dover* —3F **25**
Mt. Pleasant Clo. *Lym* —4E **17**
Mt. Pleasant Rd. *Folk* —2B **42**
Mount Rd. *Dover* —6A **24**
Mounts Clo. *Deal* —6E **5**
Mount St. *Hythe* —5E **39**
Moyle Ct. *Hythe* —6E **39**
Moyle Tower Rd. *Hythe* —6E **39**
Myrtle Rd. *Folk* —1C **42**

Nailbourne Ct. *Lym* —4E **1**
Naildown Clo. *Hythe* —4A **4**
Naildown Rd. *Hythe* —4A **4**
Namur Pl. *B Hts* —1F **25**
Napchester Rd. *Whitf* —1A
Napier Gdns. *Hythe* —6E **39**
Napier Rd. *Dover* —6B **12**
Narrabeen Rd. *Folk* —1E **41**
Naseby Av. *Folk* —2D **40**
Nash Hill. *Lym* —5E **17**
Natal Rd. *Dover* —5C **12**
Neason Ct. *Folk* —1D **42**
Neason Way. *Folk* —1D **42**
Nelson Pk. Rd. *St Mc* —1C
Nelson St. *Deal* —4H **5**
Nelson Ter. Dover —6B **12**
(off Alberta Clo.)
Neville M. *Deal* —6H **5**
Nevill Gdns. *Walm* —4F **7**
New Beach Holiday Cen. *Dy* —5E
New Bri. *Dover* —4E **25**
Newbury Clo. *Dover* —4H **2**
Newbury Clo. *Folk* —2D **40**
Newcastle La. *Ewe M* —6A
New Dover Rd. *Cap F* —5E
Newington Meadow. *Hythe* —4F
Newington Rd. *N'tn* —6A **30**
Newlands. *Whitf* —3B **12**
Newlands Dri. *Walm* —5F **7**
New Lincoln Houses. *Folk* —5B
Newlyns Meadow. *Alk* —2H
Newman Ct. *Hythe* —6G **38**
New Rd. *Elham* —2H **17**
New Rd. *Hythe* —6D **38**
New Rd. *Salt* —3D **38**
New St. *Deal* —4H **5**
New St. *Dover* —4D **24**
New St. *Folk* —2B **42**
Niagara Ho. Dover —6B **12**
(off Toronto Clo.)
Niddle St. *Deal* —4H **5**
Nightingale Av. *Hythe* —1H
Nightingale Ct. Dover —1B **2**
(off Maresfield Clo.)
Nightingale Rd. *Dover* —1C
Noah's Ark Rd. *Dover* —3A **2**
Noah's Ark Ter. *Dover* —3B
Norman Rd. *St Mb* —3F **15**
Norman St. *Dover* —3D **24**
Norman Tailyour Ho. Deal —6H
(off Hope Rd.)
Norrington Mead. *Folk* —6G
N. Barrack Rd. *Walm* —1H **7**
Northbourne Av. *Dover* —3B
Northbourne Rd. *Deal* —1A
N. Camber Way. *Dover* —2H
North Clo. *Folk* —3D **40**
North Clo. Bus. Pk. *Folk* —3D
Northcote Rd. *Deal* —6H **5**
Northcote Rd. *Kgdn* —3H **9**
North Ct. *Deal* —4G **5**
North La. *S'gte* —4E **41**
North Lea. *Deal* —4G **5**
N. Lyminge La. *Lym* —4E **17**
N. Military Rd. *Dover* —4C **2**

kin Clo. *H'nge* —1E **31**
eete Rd. *Lym* —4A **16**
ɔ La. *Alk* —1F **21**
ɔ Pas. *Dover* —4D **24**
argate St. *Dover* —5D **24**
elgrove Ho. *Dover* —3D **24**
owdrop Clo. *Folk* —5A **32**
oman Ho. *Deal* —2F **7**
nerfield Barn Ct. *S'ndge*
　　　　　—5A **26**
nerset Ct. *Walm* —2F **7**
nerset Rd. *Folk* —1E **41**
nerset Rd. *Walm* —2G **7**
ndes Rd. *Deal* —6H **5**
ιberg Clo. *Deal* —3G **5**
Bourne Rd. *Folk* —2C **42**
Camber Way. *Dover*
　　　　　—3H **25**
ιth Ct. *Deal* —5H **5**
ιthenay La. *S'ndge* —1A **26**
ιthernwood Rise. *Folk*
　　　　　—3F **41**
Goodwin Ct. *Deal* —3H **5**
ιthmead Clo. *Folk* —1G **41**
Military Rd. *Dover* —6C **24**
ιth Promenade. *Deal*
　　　　　—5H **5**
ιth Rd. *Dover* —3B **24**
ιth Rd. *Folk* —4C **40**
ιth Rd. *Hythe* —6E **39**
ιth Rd. *Kgdn* —2H **9**
ιth St. *Deal* —5H **5**
ιth St. *Folk* —2C **42**
ιth Wall. *Deal* —3E **5**
ιthwall Rd. *Deal* —5F **5**
ιnton Cres. *Hythe* —4C **38**
ιncer Ct. *S'gte* —4C **40**
ιncer Rd. *Folk* —2F **41**
ιff Coolinge La.)
ιcers Ct. *Hythe* —6E **39**
ιnney, The. *Dover* —1G **23**
ιt Ho. *Dover* —2A **24**
ιngfield Pas. *Hythe*
　　　　　—5D **38**
ιngfield Rd. *Dover* —1B **24**
ιngfield Ter. *S'ndge*
　　　　　—5B **26**
ιngfield Way. *Hythe*
　　　　　—4B **40**
ιring Ho. Flats. *Hythe*
ιff Dental St.) 　　—5E **39**
ing La. *Hythe* —3A **40**
ingside Ter. *Lym* —5E **17**
ιare, The. *Elham* —2H **17**
ιires Way. *Dover* —6A **12**
ιble Mead. *Folk* —6G **31**
ιble M. *Folk* —1F **29**
ιde St. *Hythe* —6E **39**
ιde, The. *Folk* —2C **42**
ιnbury Cres. *Folk* —6D **32**
ιnden La. *H'nge* —6B **20**
ιnhope Rd. *Deal* —5H **5**
ιnhope Rd. *Dover* —1C **24**
ιnley Clo. *Dym* —5F **45**
ιnley Rd. *Deal* —6H **5**
ιnley Rd. *Folk* —1E **41**
ιple La. *Hythe* —2B **28**
ιr La. *Folk* —6D **30**
ιtion App. *Folk* —1C **42**
ιtion App. *Mart M* —5A **8**
ιtion Dri. *Walm* —4E **7**

Station Rd. *Folk* —1F **41**
Station Rd. *Hythe* —5F **39**
Station Rd. *Lym* —5E **17**
Station Rd. *St Mc* —6A **8**
Station Rd. *Walm* —4E **7**
Stembrook. *Dover* —3D **24**
Stembrook Ct. *Dover* —3E **25**
Stephen Ct. Folk —2B **42**
(off Foord Rd.)
Stiles Clo. *Folk* —6G **31**
Stockdale Gdns. *Deal* —1G **7**
Stockham Ct. *Folk* —6E **31**
Stoddart Rd. *Folk* —1E **41**
Stombers La. *Drel* —5A **20**
Stonehall Rd. *Lyd* —1B **10**
Stone St. *N'grn* —4E **37**
Stone St. *Wnhgr* —2F **37**
(in two parts)
Stoney Path. *Walm* —1H **7**
Stonyway La. *Chu H* —6D **22**
Strand, The. *Walm* —1H **7**
Street, The. *Deal* —3A **4**
Street, The. *E Lan* —1G **13**
Street, The. *Gus* —3E **13**
Street, The. *H'nge* —6H **19**
Street, The. *Hythe* —3A **28**
Street, The. *Lymp* —5D **36**
Street, The. *Mart* —4A **8**
Street, The. *N'tn* —6A **30**
Street, The. *Shol* —6D **4**
Street, The. *W Hou* —6B **22**
Strond St. *Dover* —5D **24**
Stuart Ct. Dover —3C **24**
(off Priory Ga. Rd.)
Stuart Ho. *Deal* —6F **5**
Stuart Rd. *Folk* —1C **42**
Stub Stairs. *Chu H* —6E **23**
Studfall Clo. *Hythe* —1H **45**
Sturdy Clo. *Hythe* —5F **39**
Suffolk Gdns. *Dover* —4H **23**
Sugarloaf Wlk. *Folk* —5B **32**
Summer Clo. *Hythe* —5B **38**
Sun La. *Hythe* —5E **39**
Sunningdale Av. *Folk* —6G **31**
Sunny Bank. *Hythe* —5B **38**
Sunnyside Clo. *Ripp* —4B **6**
Sunnyside Cotts. *Deal* —5G **5**
Sunnyside Rd. *S'gte* —4D **40**
Surrenden Rd. *Folk* —1F **41**
Sussex Rd. *Folk* —1B **42**
Sutherland Clo. *Hythe* —5C **38**
Sutherland Rd. *Deal* —5G **5**
Sutton Clo. *Folk* —6G **31**
Sutton Rd. *Deal* —5A **6**
Swallow Ct. Dover —1B **24**
(off Maresfield Clo.)
Swan Grn. *S'ndge* —4B **26**
Swan La. *S'ndge* —4B **26**
Swanton La. *Lyd* —2A **10**
Sycamore Clo. *Hythe* —6A **38**
Sydcot Dri. *Deal* —3H **5**
Sydenham Rd. *Deal* —4H **5**
Sydney Rd. *Walm* —4E **7**

Tangier Clo. *B Hts* —6E **13**
Tanner's Hill. *Hythe* —3E **39**
Tanners Hill Gdns. *Hythe*
　　　　　—4E **39**
Target Firs. *Temp E* —4F **11**

Tar Path. *Deal* —5G **5**
Taswell Clo. *Dover* —3E **25**
Taswell St. *Dover* —3E **25**
Tavernors La. *Dover* —4D **24**
Taylor Rd. *Folk* —1E **41**
Teddars Leas Rd. *Etch* —2F **29**
Telegraph Rd. *Deal* —3F **7**
Telford Ct. *Folk* —1C **42**
Templar Rd. *Temp E* —4F **11**
Templar St. *Dover* —3C **24**
Temple Clo. *Temp E* —3F **11**
Temple Side. *Temp E* —4F **11**
Tennyson Pl. *Folk* —6C **32**
Thanet Gdns. *Folk* —1D **42**
Theatre St. *Hythe* —5E **39**
Theresa Rd. *Hythe* —6D **38**
Thompson Clo. *Folk* —6H **31**
Thompson Clo. *Walm* —5F **7**
Thorndike Rd. *Burm* —5A **44**
Thornebridge Rd. *Deal* —2E **7**
Thorton's La. Dover —4E **25**
(off Townwall St.)
Three Post La. *Hythe* —5E **39**
Tiber Clo. *Folk* —1C **40**
Tilbury Pl. *Walm* —4F **7**
Tile Ho., The. Hythe —5E **39**
(off Mount St.)
Tile Kiln La. *Folk* —6F **31**
Timperley Clo. *Shol* —5E **5**
Tollgate. *Deal* —1E **7**
Tolputt Ct. *Folk* —1C **42**
Tolsford Clo. *Etch* —2F **29**
Tolsford Rd. *Folk* —1D **40**
Tontine St. *Folk* —2B **42**
Tormore Pk. *Deal* —1E **7**
Toronto Clo. *Dover* —6B **12**
Tourney Clo. *Hythe* —4D **36**
Tower Ct. *S'gte* —4E **41**
Tower Gdns. *Hythe* —6E **39**
Tower Hamlets Rd. *Dover*
　　　　　—3C **24**
Tower Hamlets St. *Dover*
　　　　　—3C **24**
Tower Hill. *Dover* —3C **24**
Tower St. *Dover* —3C **24**
Townsend Farm Rd. *St Mc*
　　　　　—3D **14**
Townsend Ter. *Dover* —6B **24**
Town Wlk. *Folk* —3B **42**
Townwall St. *Dover* —4E **25**
Trafalgar Rd. *St Mc* —6D **8**
Tram Rd., The. *Folk* —2C **42**
Travers Rd. *Deal* —6E **5**
Trefor Jones Ct. Dover
　　　　　—1B **24**
Trimworth Rd. *Folk* —1F **41**
Trinity Ct. *Deal* —1E **7**
Trinity Cres. *Folk* —3H **41**
Trinity Gdns. *Folk* —3A **42**
Trinity Homes. *Deal* —4G **7**
Trinity Pl. *Deal* —1E **7**
Trinity Rd. *Folk* —3H **41**
Tudor Ho. *Deal* —6E **5**
Tudor Rd. *Folk* —1D **40**
Turketel Rd. *Folk* —2G **41**
Turner Ct. *Folk* —2F **41**
Turnpike Clo. *Hythe* —5C **38**
Turnpike Hill. *Hythe* —4C **38**
Tweed Ter. *Hythe* —5C **38**
Twiss Av. *Hythe* —5F **39**
Twiss Gro. *Hythe* —5F **39**

Twiss Rd. *Hythe* —5F **39**
Tyson Rd. *Folk* —6C **32**

Uden Rd. *Dym* —5E **45**
Undercliff. *S'gte* —4E **41**
Undercliffe Rd. *Kgdn* —2H **9**
Underdown Rd. *Dover* —4B **24**
Underhill Cotts. *Peene* —5B **30**
Underhill Rd. *Folk* —2B **40**
Underwood. *H'nge* —5A **20**
Underwood Gdns. *Folk* —4F **41**
Union Rd. *Deal* —5G **5**
Union St. *Dover* —5D **24**
Uphill. *H'nge* —1H **31**
Up. Corniche. *S'gte* —4C **40**
Up. Malthouse Hill. *Hythe*
　　　　　—5D **38**
Upper Rd. *Dover* —2E **25**
Upper Rd. *St Mc* —6B **14**
Upper St. *Kgdn* —2G **9**
Upton Clo. *Folk* —6G **31**

Valebrook Clo. *Folk* —2C **40**
Vale Rd. *Sutt* —6A **6**
Valestone Clo. *Hythe* —3B **40**
Vale View. *St Mc* —2D **14**
Vale View Rd. *Dover* —4B **24**
Valley Cotts. *Alk* —2G **21**
Valley Rd. *Dover* —6G **11**
Valley Rd. *Elham* —1H **17**
Valley Rd. *S'gte* —3E **41**
Valley Wlk. *Hythe* —4B **40**
(in two parts)
Vancouver Rd. *Dover* —6C **12**
Varne Pl. *Folk* —1D **42**
Varne Rd. *Folk* —2D **42**
Vernon Pl. *Deal* —3H **5**
Viaduct, The. *Dover* —6D **24**
Vicarage La. *Elham* —2H **17**
Vicarage La. *Shol* —6D **4**
Vicarage La. *St Mc* —3D **14**
Vicarage Rd. *S'gte* —4F **41**
Vickers Clo. *H'nge* —1G **31**
Victoria Av. *Hythe* —5D **38**
Victoria Av. *St Mb* —3F **15**
Victoria Cres. *Dover* —3C **24**
Victoria Gro. *Folk* —2B **42**
Victoria Gro. *Hythe* —5B **40**
Victoria M. *Deal* —5G **5**
Victoria M. Dover —2B **24**
(off Victoria St.)
Victoria M. Folk —3A **42**
(off Christ Chu. Rd.)
Victoria Pde. *Deal* —6H **5**
Victoria Pk. *Dover* —3E **25**
Victoria Pk. M. Dover —3E **25**
(off Victoria Pk.)
Victoria Pl. *Salt* —3D **38**
Victoria Rd. *Cap F* —3F **33**
Victoria Rd. *Deal* —6H **5**
Victoria Rd. *Folk* —2A **42**
Victoria Rd. *Hythe* —6E **39**
Victoria Rd. *Kgdn* —4F **9**
(in two parts)
Victoria St. *Dover* —2B **24**
Victoria Ter. *Hythe* —5B **40**
Victory Rd. *St Mc* —1C **14**
Vigar Pl. *Folk* —6H **31**
Villiers Ct. *Dover* —4C **24**

A-Z Folkestone & Dover 55